The Grocer's Wives

Isobel Greenshields

ISBN: 978-0-244-05177-8

Cover image: Maidenhead by Phil Dollin
copyright Judges of Hastings
www.judgesampson.co.uk

PublishNation
www.publishnation.co.uk

This book is written for my grandchildren, our future.

Table of Contents

Introduction

This is a wide-ranging family and social history seen through the eyes of a Berkshire ploughboy who seeks a better life in fashionable Maidenhead.

It touches on the Boer War, the Great War, Dunkirk and World War II.

It covers the poverty and wealth, the social divide and the need to retain respectability.

The post war period is touched on with the move to more equality and justice but through it all runs the themes of family and the need for love.

Prologue

Miss Poupard

Shortly after the last Christmas at which she provided presents for the poor of the town, Miss Poupard, spinster of the Parish of St Mary's Maidenhead, was laid to rest beside her parents. Great and genuine was the grief which greeted the news of her death, particularly in the tenements which were known as the Barracks. The lady's charitable actions had stemmed from the very finest of Christian emotions, pure unselfish compassion for those less fortunate than herself. All of her actions were carried out with discretion. The gifts had always been modest but were given from the heart, token gifts for the children and small amounts of nice groceries for the mothers.

The brutish and often desperate fathers sensed her kindness and appreciated what she did for their families, they knew that it was her own money which provided this Christmas cheer and as she never preached or scolded she was always greeted by men, women and particularly children with genuine warmth and joy.

So the occasion of her funeral was one of great sadness for the town. The front pews of the church were filled with the great and the good of the county and the back of the church was packed with the poor, standing huddled together in their real and often audible grief. Somewhere in between sat the tradesmen, amongst them Tommy Badnell, his wife, his sister-in-law and his two children. Much was made in the eulogy of the lady's charitable efforts but no mention was made of whom she had asked to carry on the work.

For the last half hour or so of the service, Tommy Badnell thought that someone might snatch the Holy Grail from him, before he had time to claim it. Someone else might well see this charitable work as a passport to civic fame and recognition. Tommy needed to be mayor, it was the one thing that would make them love him, or at the very least – respect him. He had to move quickly. He had to be Father Christmas. Not only would Nellie, Ada and Kathleen love

1

him, so would the whole town. He would show them. He twisted his moustache, always a sign of anxious thought and decided upon a plan of action: a risky one, but a plan none the less.

As the late and lamented Miss Poupard was a public figure, it was felt necessary by the ladies of the town to put on a wake. The lady was a spinster with no close relative to organise or finance any kind of reception. The ladies of the church had therefore taken it upon themselves to organise pots of scalding tea, greatly appreciated in the appalling February weather, and piles of very substantial ham and cheese sandwiches. Large Dundee cakes were also the order of the day. It was very evident, thought Nellie as she declined the offer of a sandwich, that she had not been asked to cut the bread. Anyone who had trained as a parlour maid would never have dreamt of producing sandwiches like these. A few of the men pulled out hip flasks and handed them around to keep out the cold. Tommy took out his snuff box and tapping the top of the yellow wooden box with the charming Victorian joke on it; he opened the box and offered it to the men standing nearby. There was little inter-mingling between the social groups but a few of the kindlier tradesfolk ruffled the hair of the poorer children and a few more ventured to pass the time of day with the great and the good.

Tommy Badnell, the grocer, was one of these.

"Afternoon Vicar," he beamed, "Greatly missed, greatly missed: Miss Poupard."

"Indeed Badnell." Replied the Vicar, not too condescendingly, for the man was quite generous to the church and one never knew, he might even be (though God forbid) mayor of the town one day. The Vicar gestured to a small crowd of Barracks people grouped together and eagerly munching ham sandwiches,

"Don't know what will happen next Christmas to those poor souls, now they really will miss the dear lady, they certainly will."

"The lady in fact has taken steps," said Tommy, twirling his moustache and sticking out his chest, "I do not think that the children will go without."

The Vicar leaned forwards, "You know of some bequest she made? A trust? I really am surprised she did not tell me. I feel sure she would want the church to distribute funds and administer any

2

trust. I am indeed most surprised that if she has made provision as you say, that I was not made privy to her plans."

Tommy remembered to speak softly to make people listen. He beckoned confidentially to the Vicar and whispered, "She came to see me last year - asked me to carry on her work, agreed, real honour, how could I refuse?"

The Vicar looked stunned then lifted his hand and slapped the grocer on the shoulder, "Well done Badnell, well done! You said you'd do it for the lady. Do you hear that everyone? Mr Badnell is taking over Miss P's work! We have a new Father Christmas. Well done!"

He slapped him on the shoulder again and was followed by others. Tommy stood in the chill of the church hall and basked.

The warmth of Miss Poupard's mantle was warmer than Nellie's new Russian lamb coat from Debenham and Freebody's.

Chapter 1

The Visit

It had started on one of those depressing afternoons which come so often to the Thames Valley in autumn. It was damp, the mist which drifted up from the river, past the houses of the poor, across the colonnade and up to the end of the High Street carried cold damp. It smelled of the river and penetrated all but the thickest of clothing.

Like Cambridge and other riverside towns, Maidenhead in the summer can be a delight, when the sun ricochets off the water and dances on the bricks and stones of the bridges. Then, in the days of regattas and boating parties with young women in flimsy dresses and children with fishing nets, the riverside all along the Thames becomes a social delight. For, as the song says: *'there is nothing like messing about on the river'*, well, almost nothing. But in autumn the river is dark and any activity a necessity. The punts are laid up and the beautiful people are gone to London where cosy flats are more suitable than damp and chilly houses built mainly for the joys of warmer weather.

Milly White just knew that she was cold, very cold. There was a gap between her socks, which wouldn't stay up, and her coat. Not that her coat kept her warm, it had been cheap when new and now all of the warmth was worn out of it. Milly was its fifth owner, not really owner, but wearer. Nothing in the White household was really owned by anyone, it was just whoever was going out found a coat that nearly fitted. This one nearly fitted Milly. She peered through the glass of the shop window. She didn't let go of the pram handle. Milly's whole life seemed to consist of holding onto the pram handle. In a way, she liked it, for as long as the pram was there, her mum couldn't be far away. Milly never questioned why there was always a new baby to put into the pram and cry all night and make her dad even more bad-tempered than ever, but there always was, and Milly, like her mum, always managed to love them.

Milly was watching the shopkeeper, Mr Badnell. Sometimes Mr Badnell was in a good mood and would parcel up a really good pile of bacon ends and bits and pieces and see her mum to the door, just like he did with the posh ladies. Milly liked that. Sometimes it was even better and he would say, "And this is for you little lady".

Milly liked that even more, 'little lady' was something she was not often called and when she was called it and given a bag of broken biscuits at the same time, well then she felt so good that she forgot to be cold. Forgot that her shoes pinched and that her dad was in the sort of permanently bad mood that men who are always out of work always are in and which causes them to shout at their wives and hit out at their children because it is the only way of saying what they want to say and relieving all the feelings of not being able to do what they want to do. Sometimes of course, Mr Badnell was in a bad mood, like all men sometimes were and then they didn't go in. Women like Mrs White were expert at recognising men in bad moods. Today was one of those special days for Milly; her mum came to the door closely followed by Mr Badnell. On his way past the biscuit tins he reached into one and as he opened the door said,

"And this is for you little lady, for being a good girl and minding the baby." He handed over the biscuits and his eyes went a funny watery sort of colour. Milly couldn't imagine why.

Milly and Mrs White were not the only visitors who Tommy Badnell had that day. Another sad and bedraggled figure had slipped into the shop earlier in the day, just before they closed for lunch. Miss Poupard was thin, white and haggard: not through years of childbearing and poor nutrition, but because she was ill; in fact she was dying. Miss Poupard had a growth; nothing would stop it growing, it drained more of her strength than any baby would have done and now she had to face defeat. This would be her last Christmas of delivering, hugging, weeping and rejoicing as her gifts: such small and insignificant gifts; were unwrapped, felt, held up, admired, rubbed against the face and held against the recipient as if no other article on the face of the earth were as precious.

"Oh Miss, Oh Miss!" went up the cries, and each year she knew it was all worthwhile: the planning, the saving; as even for her, a woman of her means, a little saving was necessary; but it was all worthwhile when she saw those faces wreathed in smiles. Happy for at least one day of the year - the day all children should be happy - Christmas Day. It was this realisation: the fact that the Milly Whites and the dear little Trillos would only have one more Christmas with presents and with a little special food, which brought Miss Poupard to Mr Badnell's Grocery Store.

Miss Poupard had very mixed feelings about Mr Badnell. She knew that never having married, she was an innocent in many ways, but being unmarried had given her the opportunity to observe others in a disinterested manner. She realised that the kindest women often make the worst mothers and the most beautiful women often failed to keep the interest of their men. People, Miss Poupard had learnt, were perverse; they were not predictable like animals. One thing that Miss Poupard had learned was that too much of anything is a bad thing. Her father had taught her that an overfed pony or dog does not love you any more, it just becomes lazy and ill; and her mother had taught her that overindulgence ruins the complexion and spreads the waistline.

Mr Badnell, Miss Poupard decided, was the sort of man who might well be tempted to 'overdo' it. Rumour had it that he overdid it in his personal life, but no-one really knew. Certainly the story was credible: that he had taken in his wife's widowed sister and her two small girls; but no-one really knew much of the widow's late husband, where he came from or how he died. And once, when she went up the stairs to pay her bill, they were there together and she could have sworn... but no, these were unkind thoughts and she sought to put them from her mind.

It was strange that someone she had come to regard as an annoying, arrogant and really rather nasty man at times should have been so intuitive. As she opened the shop door, the grocer had come directly from behind the bacon counter opposite and conducted her to the back of the shop. Once she was seated on a bent cane chair and he had sat himself down on a sack of soda opposite to her he had said,

"And how may I help you dear lady?" as if for once he had been able to summon up all the tact and breeding he had and had used it all at once on this special occasion.

It was strange how easy it was to tell him of her concerns for the Barracks children and their mothers, terrorised as they often were by

6

brutish men permanently out of work, bitter and free with their hands and their belts.

In fact, Miss Poupard could easily have gone on talking to the grocer about his time in Italy during the war and how he had seen the poor suffer in that beautiful country. She had started to warm to him quite unexpectedly, but their talk had been cut short by the shopkeeper having a problem with his eye. However, as he saw her to the door, his old persona resurfaced: he opened the door with a flourish, waved her through it, closed the door behind her with a loud ring and watched her progress up the High Street whilst twirling his ridiculous moustache which managed to stand completely vertical at the ends.

This was the sort of thing that worried her about the wretched man's ability to carry on her work, he would overdo it like his ghastly concerts at the Town Hall. These concerts really were dreadful. She had been to one or two but had used poor health to escape the last few, quite correctly as it happened. The concerts were always for a good cause: soldiers' widows, retired cart horses and other suitably sentimental causes; for people like Mr Badnell never noticed the very real needs which surrounded them. Most of the population of the town seemed to enjoy the 'do's' which he put on and certainly they were well attended. But what possessed people like Lady Black to attend his BTR's Olde Tyme dances she could never understand though she had to admit the man had energy and enthusiasm which is why she had gone to him with her problem.

Once Miss Poupard was sitting down in her comfortable chair at home, she went over the brief albeit successful meeting. Whatever she may have thought of the town's grocer, his response to her request had been more immediate, more enthusiastic and more compassionate than she had ever dared to hope.

"Mr Badnell," she had said, "as you know I have tried to enhance the last few Christmases for the families in the Barracks but now I find …" Amazingly he had replied very gently,

"But now due to ill health you find you cannot continue." It was all so simple, "and you would like me to carry on?"

Tommy could hardly keep his tears back. He remembered Miss Poupard as a fine handsome woman, lady in fact, who had kept the most select dress shop in the town on the corner of Old Post Office

Lane. A shop patronised by the most discerning of Maidenhead's ladies. Fashions from London and Paris were brought in to adorn the visitors who came down from London for the Season and Miss Poupard herself had worn them so well, with such elegance. In those days, the nearest the likes of Tommy got to speaking with the lady who was now sitting with him was to doff his hat if they met; a creature of such refinement and elegance, men simply turned to watch her pass. Now she was sitting opposite him, thin, ill, with her beautiful coat hanging from her bent shoulders, sitting at the back of his shop and asking a favour of him and he was so glad to comply with her request for so many reasons.

So, it had all been agreed. She had handed on one of the most important things in her life in a few moments to a man she had never really liked or approved of, simply because for all his faults, she knew he was the one person in the town who could, and would do it: the children would have their presents, the mothers would have their little boxes of groceries and perhaps for at least a few years, some of them would remember that it was she who had started the tradition. Then more than likely they would all forget, but in some measure she had given some happiness in her life, that had been her reward; and perhaps Mr Tommy Badnell would also gain from the task which she had laid upon him. But she would never know.

The pain became worse than usual and she took a measure of the morphine which the doctor had prepared for her. She had tried to avoid taking it up until then, but now that there was someone else to carry the load, she didn't concern herself; no-one would remember her. She was a spinster of this parish who, like so many others, would join her dear parents in the cemetery and that would be the end of it... and as the morphine worked its way through the pain and through her thoughts, she didn't mind at all.

Chapter 2

Breaking The News

Tommy Badnell was pleased with the outcome of the day. For a long time he had had a secret ambition: he wanted to be mayor, the mayor of Maidenhead. He could see no reason why this should not come about in the near future, for in his own mind he had all that was necessary to achieve the honour. He was a successful businessman who not only managed the most prestigious grocery store in the town, but who also, with his brother John, ran several other businesses and he owned an increasing amount of property. He was, he reflected, at quite an early age, a man of substance and a little recognition was long overdue.

He knew of course that a great many people sneered at the concerts which he put on at the Town Hall, aided and abetted by his friend Bill Pragnell; but whatever the hoity-toity members of the town may think; he had raised hundreds of pounds for good causes. He liked to stand on the Town Hall stage and recite the poems he had learned in his youth: How the Horiatii Held the Bridge, The Charge of the Light Brigade, and his favourite: Excelsior. They were all proper poems in his view with good stories. Often several people in the audience were in tears. He also liked to get the latest song sheets to keep up to date. One of his favourites was 'Long years ago out in the wilds of Australia.' He had to send away for the song sheet but it was worth it: it had adventure, sentiment and patriotism and the good people of Maidenhead loved it. It was of course also a very difficult song to perform: there was almost no tune to the verse and he needed to practise to get it just right; to get it dramatic and to carry the audience along with him.

He would retire to the cellar each evening for some weeks before the concerts and leaning against the heavy table where he boned the sides of bacon, he would close his eyes, lift up his chin and practise. Sometimes he would take a pinch of snuff from the box with the chick emerging from the egg and the caption: 'Does your mother know you're out?' That always amused him. The snuff cleared his head and helped him to think, and sing. With only the crates of Johnny Walker Red Label, Worthington White Label and a statue of the Sandeman to witness his efforts, he practised until he felt that he was perfect.

'Long years ago,
Out in the wilds of Australia,
Out in the gold-fields there once stood a camp,
Miners were gathered from all sorts and classes,
Many a scapegoat and many a scamp.
Then into their midst came a young man from England,
With him he brought a small bird in a cage,
Miners they gathered from all sorts and classes
To hear that bird sing it became all the rage.'

By the time that he sang it at the Town Hall he was word perfect and everyone was enthralled and attentive. When he got to the lines:

'There fell a deep hush,
As the song of the thrush,
Was heard by that motley crew,'

He swayed and indicated to the audience that they should join in. He really liked it when they did:

'And eyes lighted up with a bright yearning look,
As the song of that bird was heard.'

When they got to the ending:

'They thought of old England
Afar o'er the sea,
Thousands of miles away.'

There was hardly a dry eye in the house.

Now he saw the opportunity to raise the status of all these activities; he was taking over the life's work of a dying woman and a dying woman who was commonly regarded as the next best thing to a saint in the town, no-one would be able to jeer now. No-one would be able to say: *'Good old Tommy'* and then laugh as they had when he had missed being mayor last time around. No. The fact that Miss Poupard had seen fit to entrust him with her work would surely make everyone respect him, for she certainly was one of the most respected, as well as loved, women in the town. Of course. he would never be gentry like Miss Poupard. He would have to remember that

10

gentry never shouted. He had noticed that; they always spoke quietly and rather slowly, that way you had to come close and listen hard. He had tried it today and it had worked. Miss Poupard had spoken to him almost like an equal. He would have liked to have gone on talking to her but he had come over all weepy. Why did he come over all weepy he wondered? It was only since he had come back from the war.

The thought of the war banished all the pleasing and successful thoughts which he had been having up until then: Italy and all that he had seen there; all the poverty and all the beauty. He had left it behind and for what: a wife who had run the business more successfully than he had ever done, a mistress who had found other admirers in his absence and a small daughter who screamed at the sight of him. The three of them had all become so posh in the years he was away. Nellie, his wife, had been taken up by some of the wealthy ladies who had moved down from London. She bought clothes from Debenham and Freebody and sometimes went to the theatre.

Both Nellie and Ada had become friendly with Auntie Blossie who lived in the flat next door. Before her marriage she had been a high-class milliner, working in London, and now she made glorious hats for a favoured few ladies in the town. Nellie and Ada were among the favoured. Nellie had one wonderful hat with cherries that peeped out from beneath the brim; they looked so real, so delicious, that anyone who saw them wanted to reach out and pick them to taste. It was certainly a most tempting hat thought Tommy, but Nellie being Nellie, seemed unaware of the full allure of her latest headwear.

Tommy wondered if his safe return from the war was what any of them had really wanted. Still, he thought, they were just going to have to put up with it and once he was mayor they might even be pleased he was home.

His problem now was to break the news in the best possible way to them all. More than once, his sister-in-law had pointed out that whilst he got all the fun and glory, it was others who had all the work. Certainly even with two women there was a lot of work. The tiny flat housed not only himself and his own family, but also his sister-in-law and her daughter, Gladys. Not that he had ever resented

11

any of them being there. The two girls were never any trouble and Ada, well; quite simply, Ada was the love of his life.

Somehow, he could never quite come to terms with the fact that any of it was wrong. It never seemed wrong, especially after Nellie knew. He didn't want to think about it... so much he didn't want to think about. He had treated Nellie badly. A lot of people knew and even more suspected. He didn't mind about most people or what they thought, but her dad knew and that did upset him.

Old Walter Gardner wasn't gentry. He was what everyone called 'one of nature's gentlemen.' Old Walter would never have thought of sleeping with anyone but his wife. Even when she had died, he was offended and horrified at the very idea of marrying again. Old Walter had never wanted his beautiful daughter to marry a country boy like Tommy who had made his first money from horse-trading and who had a worryingly gypsy-ish look about him. Nellie was genteel like her parents, beautiful in a soft and rose-like way with warm brown hair and creamy skin and she always wore the most wonderful hats.

He had gone over all of this before and now he wanted to put it from his mind. He wanted to remember and enjoy the success of the day, the way he, Tommy Badnell, little Tommy from Knowl Hill, had been asked to take over Miss Poupard's charity work. She had come to him because she could trust him and he wouldn't let her down. He would show them. He would make it even better than it had been. He would hold concerts and raffles. The kids wouldn't have just hair ribbons and sweets, they would have proper presents like his Phil and Kath: dollies and fire-engines; books; those toys where they built houses that had little roofs and proper doors. That little Milly he had seen today, she deserved something nice, the sort of thing little girls liked. His mind ran on, planning and dreaming. Of course Miss Poupard had said that they didn't need too much, that they would be happy with simple things. But why should they be, when he, Tommy Badnell, mayor-in-waiting, was running it?

Thinking about it of course he realised that he should have taken it over long ago. He shouldn't have waited to be asked, he should have offered. Then the poor kids would have been getting decent presents years ago. But he had not. So now he must make up for lost time. The coming Christmas would still be done by Miss P. but he must start planning now for the Christmas after that. Intelligence work must be done, lists of children, their names and ages must be made. The enormity of the task he had taken on began to dawn on him, but of course Nellie and Ada would want to help him and Kathleen, surely, she would want to help? Well she certainly would help if her beloved auntie told her to. All he had to do was convince Ada – and Ada was not always so easy to convince, especially now that she had a new admirer.

He could never work out why it was that everyone wanted to be with Ada - and they did, there was no denying it. In so many ways she was just like his wife Nellie and yet in other ways she was so unlike her. If he was honest, the biggest difference in the two women was that one hated sex and the other enjoyed it. One was like a cold board just fished out of the river and the other was like… he couldn't quite decide whether it was: a feather bed; a sleep in a deep haystack on a summer's day; or quite what lovely comparison, because just then he heard them all coming up the stairs.

No-one could come up the stairs quietly; they curved in a dangerous left-hand bend from the back of the shop up to the tiny landing which gave entry to the flat over the shop in which they all lived. It often seemed silly for them all to live in such cramped quarters when he owned other more pleasant houses around the town, but it was handy to live above the shop and Tommy liked the extra rent money. He had seen too many old folk destitute. This was not going to happen to him, or Nellie, he added as an afterthought.

The three at last got through the door. It took time because the landing was so small that three people could not stand on it at the same time. Also, the door which led into the living room could only open part way due to the coats, hats and bags hung behind it. They were shorter of space than any other commodity in that tiny flat.

The jovial demeanour of the three female members of the family quietened when they saw 'Father' sitting in his chair. Nellie immediately did what he hated most and went into a great apology about the tea not being ready, how they had just been to see their dad and that she would immediately cut the bread and butter. Ada went straight to the sink and filled the kettle and Kath went beneath the table to talk to the dog. All he wanted to do was tell them, tell them his news, but despite their concerns for the tea being later than its usual prompt six o'clock, they managed to exclude him. Tommy may

13

well have been the lover of both of the women in the kitchen but he knew that the bond which counted most was the bond between them. They had been sisters all their lives, only a year separated them and they had shared a bed as girls for longer than either of them had shared a bed with any man.

Tommy may have been the boss on the surface, the money may all have been in his name, but he knew where the power really lay. The power belonged to the women who knew more about the business, more about the children - his children - and more about him than he would ever know. If this new venture was to be a success, he had to have their support; if they went against him, it would fail. He hated to admit it but he also knew that their judgement was usually sound. Nellie knew which foods sold well; she knew which customers paid their bills, which ones had the money and had genuinely forgotten and those who never could pay. She could pick out the resting actors straight away and would always tell 'the boy' to wait for the money when asked to send around a bottle of the best whisky. Quite frequently those customers who had successfully managed to have a 'bottle of the best, sent around on account', found that when the order was taken by Mrs Badnell, only half a bottle of what tasted like the worst was sent around and the wretched boy would stand outside saying things like: "Miss Badnell says I'm to get the cash. No, she don't want no cheque. I'm to get the proper money. She says she can't put it on the bill 'cause it's too big already."

Nellie came from London. Posh voices and fur coats didn't fool her. Ada had worked for an actress, a proper one; she knew them when they were on their uppers. All the same, he decided, this was his project. This was going to be his bit of glory. Of course, thought Tommy, he would need them to help out a bit. Surely that was why a man married, to have a bit of help when he needed it. But this was his pigeon and he was going to see that everyone knew it was he who was going to cook it.

It had not escaped his notice that when Mr Breed from Head Office came down to audit the books, he always spoke to Nellie as if she was the Manager and not him. Nor had he overlooked the fact that references were always made about how well his wife had coped alone, running the shop, as if they hadn't realised that he was away, serving God, King and country. Since he had come back from Italy, from the war, things just hadn't been the same.

He knew now that he hadn't really been welcomed back. They had all changed, got cocky somehow. That was it: cocky, sure of themselves and snooty with it. Somehow, he couldn't catch up with them: not in the business; or with their new friends, the way they talked and acted. Somehow, he didn't know how, they always agreed with him, waited on him, went about as they had always done; but, and he knew this now, they were the bosses. Something had happened whilst he was in Italy. He had become not only unnecessary but also unwelcome in his own home. So he had to show them. He had to put his foot down and show he could become important, admired and a strong candidate for mayor.

Nellie put the bread and butter on the table. He had never known anyone who could cut bread and butter that thinly before. She was closely followed by Ada with the tea pot in one hand and a large fruit cake in the other. He hadn't really noticed the table being laid, he supposed Kathleen had laid it without him noticing.

"Tom, a piece of bread and butter, aren't you hungry?"

He still wasn't really in the tiny room above the shop. He was wearing a Father Christmas outfit with a mayoral chain over it. He was waving from the balcony over the shop …

"Tom, are you off your food? Have some strawberry jam. Kath, give your dad some strawberry jam."

Grudgingly Kathleen pushed the cut-glass jam-jar across to him. It was no good. He simply could not stand the girl. She made herself out to be so shy and clingy to her aunt and mother but somehow she looked down on him. She was superior, or thought she was: the way they all were now, since the war, since he'd gone away to Italy, beautiful Italy where the women …. The tears, those wretched tears that always welled up and made him look a fool, were coming again. But then, when he remembered what he had lost, what he had left behind in the mountains of Italy, he knew the thoughts would never leave him. Part of him, the best part, would always be there in the poverty, in the life, the sun the warmth … the incredible beauty.

He wasn't, he was in Maidenhead and Ada was still speaking, "Tom, just what is the matter? Are you sure you didn't get shell-shocked or anything?"

Well he might as well have been: shocked; shown another world. Shown a world where women were good, loving but not prissy, saying one thing and meaning another. He was sick of all the pretence, of lying to everyone, most of all to himself. He knew that if he could think of a way of returning, he would. He would leave them all: the wife he had loved, until he had come to love her sister even more; he would leave the child who was conceived to keep him from the war but had failed in that purpose and who now seemed to have formed a total barrier between him and Ada. He would leave them all if he could. Why on earth did he stay in Maidenhead, a town that had seemed the zenith of his ambitions but which now seemed damp, crowded and grey? The women were corseted, cold and stiff. In Italy… in Italy things were different there.

"Tom, what is the matter?" Ada's voice was insistent. "Tom, do tell us what is on your mind?" They were looking genuinely concerned.

"Yes dear, tell us what the problem is." This time it was Nellie, Nellie with the sweet voice and smile. He did wish that he still loved her, so he gave her a little smile in return and put down his knife and pushed away his cup.

"I've something to tell you all," he began.

"Do I have to stay and listen?" asked Kath.

"Yes, you do," the smile had gone. Things were going wrong already. "Yes, Kath dear," he started again, "I am going to need your help. We have been entrusted with a very important task. Something for the town, something very important," he repeated lamely.

"Oh, I bet we've got to clear out the yard again," began the girl, "Clean out the yard and all the rats will run about and everyone knows they all come from the butchers. I really hate clearing up the yard. Why can't the errand boys do it?"

Tommy decided that it was now or never.

"Be quiet Kathleen! Nellie, for God's sake keep that child quiet! Miss Poupard came to see me today. Miss Poupard has asked me, us, to carry out her work and take the Barracks children their Christmas presents on Christmas Day."

The three females of the family looked back as if he had just stated that the fly-paper needed to be changed.

16

"Oh, that's alright dear," said his wife, "they don't need a lot. A few little bars of chocolate and a few hair-ribbons will keep a smile on their faces. We'll get that sorted out." She smiled again as if to say that she and her sister were capable women. Women who had managed the shop and supervised its prosperity whilst he had been away, doing whatever it was men did in times of war. They were capable. They could do anything that he could. Nellie smiled at her sister as much to say, 'Well we humour him in everything else, we may as well in this'.

"Don't worry Tom; we'll sort it all out." Ada offered this as she gathered up the tea things and took them out into the small scullery. "We'll do it; and you'll help too Kathleen," she said firmly.

"It won't be until next year," said Tommy, "So we've plenty of time."

It had been a good day. Despite everything, he had got them to agree to help him with his project but of course, as yet, they had no idea of the scale on which he wanted to carry it out. However, this was not the time to tell them about the money raising, the concerts and raffles. They had another few months to think that all they had to do was buy a few ribbons and a couple of colouring books. But he, Tommy Badnell, mayor-in-waiting of Maidenhead, knew that from next year things were going to be different.

Chapter 3

The Early Years

People frequently commented on Tommy's immaculate spelling. He liked to tell people how he came to be able to read anything and spell anything, the story may only have been partly true, but it certainly brought about a smile when he told the story.

As a young boy, Tommy had always known that the life of a ploughboy was not for him. There were days when following a plough could be almost bearable. Days when the sun shone and the birds swooped to see what delights the plough had unearthed for them. But for every day like that there were weeks of bitter, biting winds when your hands swelled up with the cold and you could barely feel your feet. Tommy would have liked to stay on at school. For some reason the teachers seemed to take an interest in him; they praised his ability to spell and his facility to add up long columns of figures accurately. Tommy's hand was always one of the first to go up in the classroom. Tommy's mother knew he was bright. He knew quite enough, she decided. He could read stories out of the Bible. So without consulting anyone she got him a job ploughing; the only job for a young lad in the countryside. He was so bored, as he told people when he related the story much later.

"Who wants to spend their life looking up a horse's arse?"

Tommy decided that horses' arses looked a lot better when they had a song sheet tied to their tails. He was able to buy song sheets which had the words to the latest music hall songs printed on them. They often had pictures of the artiste who sang the songs on the front: people like Marie Lloyd, and inside would be the words and the music. Tommy would have loved to be able to read music but there was no-one to teach him. He did ask the church organist one day who said that if the notes (he meant the little dots like tadpoles) went up, your voice had to go up and when they went down your voice went down. For a while the organist had thought he might offer to give Tommy free lessons. There was the chance that he may have a successor in the young lad. However, when he realised that the wretched boy wanted to learn music in order to sing music hall songs, he quickly put his magnanimous thoughts to one side in favour of teaching his fee-paying pupils.

Now that Tommy had found a way of cheering up his working day, he felt that he hated ploughing a little less. Up and down the fields he would go, singing away, learning the words to the songs of the day and learning how to spell words like rhapsody and melancholy. Not to mention quinine and chlorodyne. He learnt about rhyme and humour, he began to understand romance and passion. His knowledge of music hall songs became impressive and his spelling improved no end but his ploughing became quite terrible; the furrows veered all over the fields as he looked at the song sheet in favour of the plough share. The horses did their best to keep straight but distracted by the unaccustomed sounds, they too swayed and swerved with no-one to restrain them.

The farmer was not happy and told Tommy's mother that, just as he had thought, the lad was far too young to be out ploughing. He could scare the birds from the fruit trees and the crops but he was just too small for ploughing. Tommy's mother was furious for a valuable wage was lost just when she had invested in two new pairs of corduroy trousers for him. She clouted him around the head and shoulders whenever she could catch him for some time after that.

Nonetheless, the next time she went into Maidenhead she said, "You'd best come with me Tom. You can carry the basket back if we don't get a ride and besides they say there are footpads hiding in Maidenhead Thicket. You're getting quite big now; you may as well do something useful for your keep." After a while she added menacingly, "And on the way in, there is something it is high time I showed you."

Tommy set off with his mother and they were lucky to be picked up by a carter friend. They sat on the tail board of the horse-drawn vehicle watching the road slip away under them. Tommy thought he spent an awful lot of his life looking down at fields and roads that is when he wasn't looking at horses' arses! The cart they were on was carrying bricks from the brickyard at the back of the cottage to one of the many new building sites in Maidenhead. The dust from the bricks blew over them as they moved down the road, covering them with brownish orange dust that went up their noses and into their ears. They were grateful for the lift which had saved them a walk of four or five miles.

When they got to the outskirts of the town, before they went down Castle Hill, Tommy's mother called to the carter, "You can put us down here then Jed. We're obliged for the ride but there is somewhere I want young Tom here to see. He's out of work, couldn't keep his furrows straight."

Tommy ducked in anticipation of the clout that he knew would follow this comment.

His mother got down from the back of the cart with surprising agility and plodded off. He had never been down this particular road. He had never really been anywhere except to school, church and work. He wondered where on earth she was taking him. He trotted alongside her making sure he kept to the side that she carried her basket, just in case she should decide to reach out and give him another clout for good measure.

After a short walk they came to a crossroads and across the road and to the right was a low building made of yellow brick. As they took the right-hand turning towards the town of Maidenhead, they saw a church with more buildings behind it. Even further on, behind some railings, they saw a large piece of land and working on it with hoes, spades and rakes were several very old men tending rows of cabbages and potatoes and a few rows of flowers.

Tommy's mother dropped her heavy basket and straightened her back before adjusting her bustle.

"Know what that place is Tommy?" she asked.

"Is it prison?"

"No!" the angry woman replied, "It's where they put the likes of you. It's called the Workhouse. It's where you go when you can't scrat for yourself, which is why, my fine lad, you have to work all your life and save for your old age, or you'll end up in there."

Tommy looked at the very old men hoeing their rows of cabbages. It didn't look too bad but all the same from his mother's voice he decided that the Workhouse was not where he wanted to spend his old age or indeed any other part of his life. For the rest of the journey down the steep slope of Castle Hill, his mother kept repeating,

"If you don't work, that's where you'll end up my lad. Oh yes you will, in the Workhouse."

It was almost like an incantation, over and over again, so that by the time they reached the High Street Tommy was convinced that he would be dropped off that very night at the Workhouse and would spend the rest of his life hoeing cabbages.

Life however is forgiving and just as it seemed that Tommy's life was at its worst, just when at thirteen he thought things could end in the horror of the Workhouse, life took on a merciful guise and the whole of his life changed forever, for the better.

Tommy rarely visited the town and it seemed to him exciting and full of things he had never seen before. The fruits in the greengrocers were unfamiliar, there were rows of poultry and game hanging up outside the butchers and pastries and cakes in the confectioners' window to make your mouth water. It was while he had his nose to the baker's window, while he was trying to ignore his mother telling him to come on and forget the idea of having a cake that something caught his eye. His mother would never have noticed it. She was too busy chiding, pushing and complaining, but Tommy noticed it and it was the most important thing that he was ever to notice in his whole life.

It was a small, discreet card stuck onto the window of the grocery shop next door to the confectioners and on it Tommy read,

'Young man of smart appearance and good educational standard wanted. Must be smart and clean and over fifteen.'

Tommy looked up at the sign above the door. It read in flowing gold letters on a dark green background across the top of the shop window,

'Kilbys, High Class Grocers and Off Licence, 21 High Street.'

"Mum, Mum," said Tommy, "look! That's what I want to do; I want to work somewhere like that."

Both Tom and his mother pressed their noses against the shop window. Inside were long counters with shiny brass scales. On top of a marble topped counter a brass bacon slicer faced the shop doorway and on the right of the shop entrance were rows of biscuit tins. But what took Tommy's eye most of all were the people working in the shop. They all looked clean, their hair was combed, they wore sparkling white coats and they were chatting and smiling.

"That's what I want Mum," he said, "That's what I want to do. I really want to Mum." Then looking her in the eye he continued fervently, "Please Mum, please help me to get a job in that shop."

Tommy's mother hardly knew what to say. She had a feeling that the Almighty was having a hand in this. It seemed so strange that having just frightened her son with the Workhouse, that he should see the notice. For here he was reading it out to her. He could certainly read. It would have taken her a long time to make it out. How could she help him? It said smart: he was in his old country clothes; it said clean: he was covered in dust and grime from the brick-cart ride and long walk; it said fifteen: he was two years away from fifteen.

Tom's mother may have been illiterate but she was a woman of guile and cunning. If she really wanted something, she could usually conspire to get it. How wonderful if she could get Tommy a job in the grocers, to be away from the mud, manure and rain, not to mention the farmer, she thought. He might also be able to get groceries cheaply. She looked Tommy directly in the eye and said, "We'll have to lie, Tommy."

Then to his amazement, she took him to the horse trough, dipped her shawl into the water and to the amusement of passers-by, proceeded to wash his face and hands. She spat on her hands and smoothed down his hair, peered into his ears and poked around in them for a while with her finger. Looking down she saw the mud on his boots and gave them a rub over with the now filthy shawl.

"Go on in son," she said, "say you'll bring your birth certificate tomorrow. Remember you are just fifteen, just left school."

Tommy took hold of the door handle and began to push. A terrible stab of panic gripped his lower stomach and just as he was on the point of turning, running back to his mother and risking yet another clout, he saw a man of about thirty coming towards the door. For an instant his panic gripped him, but the man on the other side of the door smiled, swung open the door and said, "Come in young man, come in. How, may I ask, can we help you?"

Mr Kilby, the owner of Kilby's Grocery store had had a difficult life. His father's bankruptcy had threatened to make any sort of business life impossible for him so he had discharged his father's dishonour and gone on to be successful and respected. He was one of the founding members of the Wimbledon croquet and lawn tennis club and he often managed to get tickets for his friends and employees to watch the tennis matches.

He had watched the episode outside the shop and was interested to see how the very young man now opening the door of his shop would react. He had been impressed at how quickly he had noticed the advertisement and that he obviously had no difficulty reading it out to his mother. He obviously came from country folk but this was not always a bad thing. The country lads were often healthier and more honest. But he did look young, no more than thirteen he would have judged... far too young, still they would see.

Tommy took off his cap and said, "I've come about the job. I mean, sir, I would like to work here, I really would Sir. I would like to work in here. I just don't know who to ask."

The poor lad's confidence seemed to evaporate and Mr Kilby, who could remember the pain of youth and the stresses and anguish which come as a result of wanting something a lot and not knowing how to get it said, "Well now, young man, you have made a good start because I am Mr Kilby and this is my shop, so you have come to the right person."

His encouragement put Tommy at his ease and he said, "I know I look a bit untidy today, but I've walked in from Knowl Hill and it's quite a long way."

"Knowl Hill? Indeed, it is a very long way. Did you come in to find a job or did you come for some other reason?"

As they talked, Mr Kilby guided Tommy to the back of the shop, away from the customers and some of the assistants who were listening and having a little chuckle at this gauche country lad. They doubted if he would get the job. Mr Kilby asked very difficult questions, the adding up questions were very hard indeed and this lad looked as if he was only about thirteen years old.

"Sit down," said Mr Kilby. "Now, first things first, tell me your name."

Tommy settled himself on an upturned crate which the older man indicated that he should use as a seat.

"It's Thomas sir. Well really, it's Richard you see but I'm called Tommy because my dad is called Richard and it gets a bit muddled. My name is Richard Thomas Badnell, but I'm known as Tommy."

"Well now Tommy," said the shop owner, "my name is Mr Kilby and you can call me that. I like it more than 'sir'."

"Sorry sir," said the boy, "Sorry Mr Kilby."

"Now, very important" said Mr Kilby, "Tell me why you want to work in my shop."

Tommy was not certain what the right answer was and he paused, looking at the dust that was drying in nasty swirls on his boots. Should he say that he didn't want to spend the rest of his life looking at a horse's arse? Should he say he wanted to leave the countryside and work in the town?

"Quickly," said his questioner, "quickly, why do you want to work here?"

Tommy looked up and said, "Because it's so clean. The aprons are so white. It's all so lovely. I just know I'd be happy here."

Mr Kilby smiled, "Well," he said, "that's a very good reason for wanting to do something. We all have the right to be happy. Did you know that Tommy?"

Tommy had always had a suspicion that people should be happy. He didn't think that his mother would agree, but now, even more, he wanted to work here. He wanted to work for someone who believed in being happy.

"Well now Tommy, let us see if you could make me happy if you worked here, because that is important too, don't you think? Now can you add up?"

Tommy smiled. Oh yes, he could add up. He was the best in the school. He could add columns of figures. He could divide and multiply and his speciality was money. He could picture the little piles of farthings and ha'pennies, the big round pennies, thre'p'ny bits, sixpences, shillings, florins and half-crowns. He rarely saw a ten shilling note or a pound but he knew how many half-crowns went to make up a pound and he knew how to add all the piles up in his head, quickly and accurately.

"Now Tommy, if someone buys half a pound of biscuits at sixpence a pound, how much would it cost?"

The answer came back immediately, and was accompanied by a look that said, 'are you insulting me?' The questions became more and more difficult and complicated. They involved giving change with three farthings, amounts with eleven pence ha'penny, but the answers came back calmly and confidently and in every case correctly. Mr Kilby was impressed. But could this young ready reckoner spell? He most certainly could. He could also write in the most beautiful copperplate handwriting. Mr Kilby was impressed yet concerned. He was not fifteen, he could tell from his voice. There was no sign whatsoever of fluff on his face, yet he was eager, he was accurate, he was hungry for the job.

"How strong are you, Tommy? Can you lift?"

Tommy thought of all the heavy water pails he had to carry, the heavy harnesses he had lifted, so he smiled when he was asked to lift a box of groceries. The secret was to bend your knees and take a deep breath before you lifted.

"Now could you lift that crate outside and put it on the pile with the others?"

Mr Kilby felt rather mean asking the boy to lift the crate of soda siphons. They came in a heavy wooden crate as the siphons were of far more value than the soda water and when the crate was full it was almost impossible to lift single-handed. He watched closely as the boy bent his knees and attempted a lift. Of course it barely moved. The lad stood and looked at it, looked at the stack of empties piled against the wall of the yard and then calmly proceeded to half empty the crate. The next time he tried to lift it, the crate was easily managed. He put it at the side of the wall and then in two short journeys, added the other siphons to the crate.

He had a look of triumph on his face as he resumed his seat.

"That was well thought out. Well done!"

To his amusement, the lad gave a sly little smile and said, "Well, Mr Kilby, my mum always says that there's more than one way of skinning a cat."

Mr Kilby was impressed. Had the boy looked a little older, he would have hired him on the spot, so he said, "If you were a little older Tommy, the job would be yours, but you are very young. Tell the truth now. You are not really fifteen now are you?"

"My mum said I can bring in my birth certificate tomorrow if you like," was the reply. He looked back at the swirls of dust on his boots and unconsciously rubbed the toe of his right boot on the back of his left trouser leg.

"Very well," said Mr Kilby, "it will give me time to think, but you can tell your mother that you are a clever lad and even if I feel I cannot employ you now, I would like to see you again in a couple of years' time."

It felt strange walking out of the shop, for Tommy just knew that was where he wanted to work for the rest of his life. He somehow knew that 21 High Street was where he was meant to be. Just as he knew he didn't want to be in the Workhouse or behind a plough, he knew that although he was too young for the job and lived far too far from the shop to get there each day that was where he was going to work - right in the middle of the High Street. He looked so confident that as his mother emerged from an alley just up the street, she thought that he had already been given the job.

"No," he said, "but I know I will get it. I answered all of his questions. He said I was to tell you that I am a clever lad and most of all he knew that I wanted it. Then as an afterthought, "And he knows I want to be happy. He believes in being happy."

Old Mrs Badnell looked at her youngest son. He was a funny lad. Perhaps a bit too sharp, she had a feeling that he might well end up cutting himself one day, but she had never thought about happiness, or sadness come to that. So, she said, "Well, that's alright then young Tom, and if you've to be back tomorrow with your birth certificate we'd best be off home for we've the certificate to see to and you'll need to see to your feet if you've to be in tomorrow."

The journey home was so different from the journey in. His mother refrained from clouting him and actually listened when he told her the questions he had been asked. Then, when he told her about the crate, how he had realised that it was a riddle and that he managed to solve it, she looked at him with something close to wonder, or could it be respect?

To Tommy's surprise, after his mother had stirred the fire and filled the kettle, she told him he could see to his feet and get an early night. She would collect the eggs and feed the hens and when he was in bed, she would change the date on the birth certificate. Although she was virtually illiterate, she was adept at forging. All of her children appeared at least two years older on their birth certificates than in fact they were. In that way, they could join the army or go into service when it was convenient for their mother.

Tommy was sent to see to his feet. This involved peeing into his chamber pot and soaking his feet in the urine. Strangely, as all country folk knew, this was very soothing and if a ploughman or a traveller did this, he rarely suffered from corns, blisters or calluses.

"If I get the job Mum, where shall I stay? It's too far to come home each night."

"You can stay with your sister, Sue," replied his mother. "She can put you up."

Tommy was not too pleased with this part of the plan for his new life. His sister Sue was not his favourite and anyway he knew that she wanted to put distance between herself and the family at Knowl Hill. She was newly married and lived by the moor. Even if she would have him, her husband might have something to say.

He was not going to think of it. He was going to think of the shop where he was going to work, where he was going to be happy. He took off his outer clothing and wearing his long johns he climbed beneath the blankets and slept immediately.

Tomorrow, Tommy had the long walk again but this time he didn't care. He would get the job. He would move to the town and being a little more precocious than he had appeared to Mr Kilby he also thought that one day he would meet the sort of lady he had seen in town that day; a lady with a pretty face, a beautiful hat and a softly curving bosom, or as he put it more bluntly in his country way, a lady with big tits.

The walk went quickly. Never had five miles seemed so short. Nearer the town, a brick cart slowed and the carter asked if he wanted to quickly hop on, but he declined the offer remembering how dusty he had got the day before. His mother had dusted off and brushed his clothes and boots as best she could and his face, hair and hands were scrubbed and polished. In his inside pocket, he had the precious scrap of paper, his newly falsified birth certificate. Tommy hoped that Mr Kilby would not notice how the three had been altered to one, for as his mother said, had he been born in 1885 it would have been easy to change it to 1883, but as he was born in 1883 it was much harder. Nonetheless, she had done a fairly good job and Tommy sincerely hoped that his mother's forgery skills would succeed in getting him the job that he wanted so much.

Fate played into Tommy's hands. Just as he was walking into town, one of Mr Kilby's most senior assistants was telling him that he had been offered the post of assistant manager at Budgens. Mr Kilby was pleased for the young man. This is how life should be. A continual improvement and change and as he was not the sort of man to hold anyone back, he congratulated the assistant, recognising the fact that when young men start walking out, there is a need for them to improve their situation. However, it would leave the shop short of good, reliable staff. Of course he had Charlie, a most promising sixteen year old, but he had hardly finished his apprenticeship. Just when he was considering how he could fill in the gap, the door opened and a shiny faced, if rather breathless youth appeared in the doorway. Of course, the lad from yesterday, back already. He must be eager. Mr Kilby had almost decided against taking him on at this time because he was undoubtedly too young, but the realisation that good help was quickly snapped up had been brought home to him that morning and now he was going to need two new members of staff.

"Come through lad," he said. "Now let's have a look at this birth certificate."

Whilst clearing his father's bankruptcy, Mr Kilby had scrutinised many papers and could see a forgery instantly.

"Does your mother know that forgery is a crime?" he asked. The boy looked back at him and answered, "I don't know."

"Well tell your mother that as I now need two assistants and as I am a very busy man, I will not report her to the police, this time."

He smiled at Tommy and said quite simply, "You have the job. Start next Monday morning, half past seven. We provide the overalls - that is if we can find one small enough for you." He then called out, "Charlie, take this young whippersnapper and give him a mug of tea and a doughnut and show him the ropes. His name is Tommy and he will be starting here next Monday."

He turned and went down the stairs to the cellar where he counted and recounted the bottles of spirits which made up so much of the value of the stock. Tommy followed the older boy to the back of the shop. He wondered how old Charlie was, seventeen at least and without altering his birth certificate. He was tall and had a pleasant easy going way about him. He wasn't shy and Tommy knew instinctively that Charlie could be trusted. He was the one to watch and follow. He was not to know at that point that Charlie was to be one of the most important influences of his life and had he followed Charlie closer and for longer, then his life would have been as successful and happy as anyone has a right to be.

Chapter 4

Sergeant Derby

From the time that he took on Miss Poupard's charity work, things began to go well for Tommy. Perhaps as the 1920's drew to an end the memories of the war began to fade in people's minds. Young Phil was growing up and Tommy was proud of him. His desire to enter the new trade of motor mechanic made Tommy think that this was where he had left off as a horse trader. They even talked about horsepower. Kath was always wrapped up in her friend Audrey and spent much of her time with the girl at Lent Rise, much healthier than always clinging to Ada.

Ada, Nellie and he had settled down to living together as best they could in the way that people who have not choice in the matter usually do. He had thought at one time that Ada, his beloved Ada would be leaving them. At about the time of Miss Poupard's death, Ada had a new admirer. There was a great shortage of eligible men after the war but Ada had managed to attract Sergeant Derby and everyone agreed that he was a fine, good-looking man and a great success with the ladies.

At one time, it seemed that whenever Tommy went up the stairs, there was Sergeant Derby, charming, polite and invariably sitting in his armchair. Sergeant Derby was confident and at ease with himself and everyone else. People said that he and Ada made a fine couple. People said that Nellie would soon need to look for a new cook, housekeeper, book-keeper and nanny. Certainly, if Ada left, things would have to change. Tommy prayed that Sergeant Derby would be drafted somewhere else; but then what if Ada were to follow? What if he was sent to India or South Africa and Ada went too? In the event, things worked out far better for Tommy than he could have hoped for. It showed him quite conclusively that the Almighty viewed his unconventional living arrangements just as he did: as sensible, economical and cosy; it was good for all three of them and as no-one outside the family knew, no-one could be hurt.

One day, whilst he was slicing bacon behind the bacon counter at the back of the shop, a woman he had never seen before came in. She was smartly dressed, pretty and very, very angry. She stood in the middle of the shop and asked very loudly, "Well, where is he?"

Nellie, as ever, believed that there was a simple explanation for everything and answered that the errand boys were all a little late with their deliveries that day as the weather had been so bad in the morning. On hearing Nellie's voice, the smart, pretty and very angry voice demanded, "Are you his fancy piece? Because if you are, I'm here to put a stop to it. I know all about it and I'm here to take him home."

She advanced towards Nellie who was smiling at her in her usual, turn-the-other-cheek manner.

"Don't look all sweet and innocent at me," she screamed, "you've stolen my husband and I'm here to get him back, you, you..."

Tommy realised who she must be, even if Nellie didn't. This had to be Mrs Sergeant Derby, wronged wife, out for vengeance. Sergeant Derby was upstairs, not paying his bill, but paying court to Ada. As swiftly and quietly as he could, Tommy slipped around the bacon counter and started to climb the stairs. He had no idea of how he could extricate the amorous Sergeant from the flat above as there was no exit apart from through the shop. Just as his rear was about to disappear from view, he heard Nellie's sweet but desperately upset voice calling,

"Tom, Tom, don't leave me with this woman. What on earth is she talking about?"

Tom turned and slowly descended the stairs.

"Tom, tell her I'm your wife. Tell her to go away."

The thought that the woman who was wronging her also had a husband, who presumably was in the know and who presumably condoned the wrongdoing, further (if it is possible) incensed the smart, pretty and incredibly angry person.

Tom went behind the biscuit counter and stood behind Nellie, putting his arm around her shoulder; it was one of the few times she felt gratitude for him.

"Madam," he said, "This is my wife, Helen, or Nellie. Neither she nor I know what you are talking about. Please explain or go away."

This stopped the woman in mid-expletive. She started to apologise, she must have the wrong shop, the wrong woman. The crowd of shoppers started to fall back to allow her to reach the door. There was silence, for all of two seconds. Then, the door to the flat was heard to open, the laughter of a man and a woman came merrily, joyfully down the stairs, followed by the bright, lively footsteps of a man in his prime; a man in his prime who is leaving the woman he loves. "I'll see you later then, Ada, as soon as I can get away."

It was never to be. Not later. Not ever. For as Sergeant Derby walked into the silent, spellbound shop, his wife advanced and hit him harder than he was ever likely to have been hit in initial training, battle or anywhere else. As far as anyone knew, he never saw Ada again, or she him. He was dragged ignominiously from the shop by his wronged wife, leaving behind a wronged sweetheart who would take a long time to forget him.

Sergeant Derby left a gap in everyone's life for he had been jolly and good-looking. In an age that never referred to men as sexy, he did have a certain way with him which was much the same. Tom was sorry for Ada, sorry for Nellie who had secretly hoped that her sister, much as she loved her, might move away but most of all, Tom felt sorry for Sergeant Derby though he was glad for himself. He enjoyed comforting Ada and reminding her that men may come and men may go but he would always be there for her.

Ada was not her usual self for a long time. She had genuinely felt for Sergeant Derby. He was the sort of man she had always wanted: good-looking, intelligent, generous, and above all, fun. Even if she was sitting at the desk, struggling with the difficulties of bills, refunds and wages, if Sergeant Derby was in the room, life was fun. He made her feel alive. He had also offered, for a short while, an escape route from this claustrophobic life into which she had walked with her two girls. This life which ensured shelter and food, company and affection was a compromise which offered no-one anything but limited happiness. True, on the surface, as Tom pointed out so often, on the practical side it worked well. Nellie, her sweet and pretty sister, worked in the shop, putting up with the customers who changed their minds, questioned bills and vowed that things had never been delivered. Nellie with her sweetness, her soft brown eyes and hair soothed and calmed them, always gave them the benefit of the doubt and never lost a customer.

Ada's domain was above stairs. She cleaned and cooked, brought up the children and kept the books, all unpaid. No wonder Tom thought it was a good arrangement. It certainly worked for him. But who else benefitted? Not her, not Nellie. Although the children were better off with her there, she decided. One of the things which had worried her when she thought of leaving with Sergeant Derby was the distress of leaving Kathleen behind. Kathleen was her niece but she loved her like a daughter.

Ada did see Sergeant Derby just once more. She and Kathleen had gone to the Rialto to see a film and during the Pathé News, when everyone was concentrating on their ice-creams and looking to see who else was in the cinema, Ada looked up at the screen to see a traditional hunt meeting. There they were, all the gentry on their horses bending down to take a stirrup cup from mine host, who happened to be Sergeant Derby. Oblivious to the rest of the picture-goers, Ada rose to her feet and called, "Kathleen, Kathleen, it's Sergeant Derby, it is, it is him."

Kathleen looked and there, sure enough, was the debonair Sergeant Derby handing up the drinks outside a beautiful country inn. Kathleen knew that Ada would have run an inn so well with Sergeant Derby and would have been happy with her long-lost sweetheart. So she gave her aunt's arm a squeeze and said she was glad that she hadn't left them. Then she pretended not to notice the tear that meandered down the older woman's face.

Chapter 5

Alice Crawford

In Kathleen, Ada recognised what she had admired in her idol: Alice Crawford. Alice Crawford was an Australian actress whom she had been lucky enough to work with when her own baby was just born. Miss Crawford had style. She was not at all like English actresses and aristocrats; she could ride bareback, drank like a man and she took lovers when she wanted them – not when they wanted her. She had no misgivings about taking on a housekeeper with a small baby.

'As long as the place is spotless and the food fantastic,' she would say. They had a wonderful time together. Ada never minded the extra work made by the parties and the house guests. She was living. This was how life should be. Of course, even the liberated Miss Crawford drew the line at a housekeeper with two children, but she was very good about it. She gave Ada a very nice parting gift. *'This should keep you going for a while,'* she had said, *'until you get on your feet.'* She had put her arms around her and said how much she would miss her. She had meant it. Both had recognised in each other a dynamic and sensual reflection of each other; one may have been a famous actress and the other a pregnant housekeeper, but there was mutual respect between them.

On leaving, Miss Crawford had uttered, *'If things get really sticky, you let me know.'*

'Very well, Miss Crawford,' she had said but she had no intention of every bringing her failures to the woman she admired so much. She would sort it out, provide for her children.

Ada would miss some of the trips she had made with Miss Crawford such as going to get her jodhpurs made and seeing Miss Crawford sitting astride the large wooden horse whilst some very intimate measurements were taken.

"It's the only way Ada," she called merrily, "this is the only place in England that makes jodhpurs that actually fit!"

Fit they did. Miss Crawford looked wonderful and Ada realised the difference then between having the best and the nearly best. There was simply no comparison. Ada knew that if ever in the future she was in need of riding gear, then Harry Hall was the place to go. She learned a lot from Miss Crawford and Ada was not one to forget.

Ada didn't really want to go over the years in between leaving Miss Crawford and sending the telegram to Nellie. She didn't want to go over the increasing desperation of trying to cope alone, knowing that help would come from several sources if only she could bury her pride and ask for it. When the girls became ill, there was no choice any longer. She had just enough money left to send a telegram. It said:

'Please meet Paddington, Thursday, noon. Ada.'

Tom had come. He had lifted the girls Mona and Gladys into the carriage. He had put her bags on the rack and sat opposite her. She had met him only once or twice before and had realised that he was attracted to her, but now, as the train slowed down over the Brunel Bridge to stop at Maidenhead Station, he took her hands in his and said,

"I love you, Ada. I know I shouldn't, but I do." Then he had leaned forwards in the carriage and kissed her on the lips before picking up the sleeping girls and stepping down onto the platform.

Nellie remained flustered about the Sergeant Derby incident for some time. It was she who had to face the customers and make the explanations. The existing situation was hard enough – living with her husband and her sister. She knew there were rumours about her husband having two wives. In fact, she really didn't care if Tom ceased to be her husband altogether. But she had made sacrifices. She had put up with the really hard times and his dreadful old witch of a mother. Now that things were going nicely, she was not about to be displaced. She liked her nice clothes and the affection with which she was held in the town. She loved her two children: young Phil, now almost a grown man and the little Kath. But Kathleen of course always wanted to be with her auntie.

If only Sergeant Derby had been single, he would have married Ada and they would have gone away. But he was already married and she had had to cope with a scene in her shop. The eczema between her eyes began to itch as it always did when she was upset.

During the war she had never had eczema; she had found that running the shop was easy. All you had to do was be pleasant to the assistants (something Tom never realised with the older male members of staff) keep the books and keep Head Office informed. Head Office had appreciated her, the gentlemen who came to audit the books were always most complimentary. Nellie had blossomed.

She couldn't believe how men made such a fuss about things. They only had to run a business whereas she had to do all the other things as well. Nonetheless she and her sister had coped. Not only that, the takings had gone up, the staff had stayed and everyone had seemed happy. That had been life as it should be, no-one scolding or bossing. She glanced towards the bacon counter. Then the war had ended and Tom had returned – bald and with a moustache that looked like barbed wire. No wonder Kathleen had screamed at the sight of him. Nellie had often wondered during the war, how she would react if he were killed. She was not prepared for her reaction when he arrived home. Her heart sank. She suddenly remembered the physical difficulties of sharing a bed, the snoring, and the lack of sleep. A feeling of utter revulsion and despondency came over her.

However, "Hello Tom," she had said with a calmness that did not reflect her mood, "Welcome home."

Chapter 6

The Preparations

Despite everything, the preparations for Christmas continued. It was fairly easy for someone of Nellie's charm to find out the ages and sex of the children in each family and Ada, with her skill at dealing with suppliers and the other retailers of the town, managed to negotiate deals and discounts on little dollies and wooden trains. McIlroys and Butlers were both persuaded to make donations of wrapping paper and tinsel. Butlers also agreed that after the store closed on Christmas Eve, their Mr Norman, who would be playing the part of Father Christmas, would bring round the costume for Mr Badnell to wear in the morning. Strangely, not only did the family get caught up in the excitement of the forthcoming project, so did the whole town. Raffle tickets had been on sale for some time, not only in Tommy and Nellie's shop but also in Bill's, the greengrocers. At this rate, each family would be able to have chocolate biscuits, a bacon joint and a small Dundee as well as the bottle of Camp coffee, packet of tea and piece of cheddar which Miss Poupard had been wont to supply. A feeling of exhilaration swept over the town.

Other parts of the world may be going through depression, but as Tommy would say puffing out his chest, *'We don't hold with depressions in Maidenhead.'*

It was during this period of euphoric self-confidence that Tommy was to make mistakes which would come to haunt him for the rest of his life. He was not unkind at heart but typical of his time and class. The men of his time and class may have been noted for many things but open-minded compassion was not one of them.

Ada had been counting the money collected through raffles and donations. She was quite meticulous in recording each farthing.

"There is an awful lot of money here," she said, "I can hardly believe how much. I think it would be a good idea to buy the dads a few whiffs. After all, it's their Christmas too."

She knew at once that she had said the wrong thing. Tommy's face thundered, "I promised woman and children, not that lot of work-shy scroungers." He ranted on, slamming doors and slamming his fist against the table. Nellie came rushing up the stairs,

"What is it? What is it?" she asked.

"Ada wants to give those scroungers at the Barracks cigars!" spat Tommy.

"Well not cigars, maybe," said Nellie, having missed the start of the argument, "but what about a few cigarettes, or whiffs even?"

The sheer frustration of the whole thing welled up inside him. He raised his hand …

"Go on," Nellie said barely whispering, "go on and you'll never see me again."

Until then he had never realised just how things had changed. Of course he should never have raised his hand to her but her reaction had shocked him. Why had she not just said: *'Don't hit me,'* or *'Calm down, Tom'*? But no, she had threatened to leave. She was quite definite. And worse, when he had looked at Ada, her stare showed exactly where her sympathy lay. She had walked across between them and put her arms around Nellie. She had excluded him. There was no need to say anything.

The shop was unsupervised and he hurried downstairs. That evening he didn't go upstairs for his tea, he took a bag of broken biscuits down to the cellar with a piece of cheddar from the cheese counter and opened a bottle of Guinness. He doubted if on this particular evening it would be good for him. Things inevitably returned to what passed as normal. When he had crept into bed that night, he saw there was a bolster the length of the bed. Nellie's back was turned towards him and when he awoke at six-thirty the next morning, she had got up, taken her clothes and dressed downstairs. They never discussed the changes, but this was to become the pattern of their marriage for the rest of their lives.

Chapter 7

The Best Christmas

By the end of November in 1929, the front parlour, the largest, but totally unused space in the flat, was becoming full of exciting parcels. The children's presents were certainly an improvement on what the blessed Miss P had managed to provide. The hampers were looking full and mouth-watering. They only awaited a sprig of holly to finish them off. Quite unexpectedly, Kath and her friend Audrey had managed to get hold of pixie outfits and they were to ride on the decorated cart to help distribute the parcels.

'When shall we get our Christmas?' Kath had asked. Ada had assured her that their Christmas would be wonderful and that when they got back from the Barracks all would be ready: their presents, their dinner, their candles.

That Christmas was undoubtedly the best that any of them ever had, ever. The cart was beautifully decorated and the man from Butler's remembered to bring around the Santa costume. Amazingly, it fitted Tommy like a glove. The girls dressed in their costumes and giggled and jumped around before climbing onto the cart.

They had a very short way to go so having gone to the trouble of decorating the cart they took the long way round. It was early but some people were about and waved to them, everyone shouting 'Happy Christmas, Happy Christmas!' By the time they entered the Barracks the people who lived there were aware that something was happening and spilled out into the square. Their faces were at first amazed and then slowly, as it dawned on them what might be... what was ... happening: their faces broke into smiles; children jumped up and down; mothers with looks of incredulity surveyed the scene: the groomed horse, the cart decked out with tinsel and red and green crepe paper; two rather large pixies and Mr Badnell, for that was who it certainly was – they could tell by the moustache which poked up above the cotton wool – all dressed up as Father Christmas.

The presents were all carefully labelled by Ada and soon every woman and child was holding a parcel. But the men lounged against the walls of the building. They smiled at the children's joy but thought that a few whiffs would not have gone amiss; after all it was said that the raffles had raised an awful lot of money. One of the women, it may have been Mrs White, called out,

"Good old Tommy."

And they all joined in and waved and sang, 'For he's a jolly good fellow.' Kath and Audrey waved back and couldn't imagine why they had not wanted to come at first. Tommy thought his heart would burst. It had happened, the sun shone and glittered on the tinsel and just then the photographer from the paper came through the arch and took their photo.

As they drove home, the vicar on this way to church called out, "Well done," and "Happy Christmas Mr Badnell, Happy Christmas girls!"

Mrs White ushered her children inside. She was sorry that Mrs James had not been able to persuade Mr Badnell to change his mind and give the men a few whiffs or a little miniature. She wondered if he realised just how left out the men all felt. They were left out all year from the normal life of the town; from the dignity of work; the camaraderie of the pub on a Friday night. There were no firm's outings for their men, no Christmas bonuses or long service watches. They were looked down on by all of the other men in the town and often with no good reason. Did they really think that all the men wanted to be at home surrounded by crying babies? Did Tommy Badnell honestly think that her hubby wouldn't like gravel pits and horses and carts if he had the chance? In any case, everyone said it was Mrs Badnell and her sister who had all the business sense. He was very good to her she knew but if only he could understand that the women and children would have a much better Christmas if only he would include the men. She gave her husband a sad little smile and asked,

"Why don't you help Milly with her dollies while I get the dinner on?" She put her arm around him and gave him a little kiss above his ear. He thought for a moment that he might give her a clout to show her not to tell him what to do but she held him against her and gave a little squeeze. So he patted her waist and went to help Milly cut out the dollies dresses and bend the little tabs over the dolls shoulder to keep them on.

As promised, Ada and Nellie had their Christmas ready. The goose, which was Ada's choice, was cooking in a sea of grease in the oven, the vegetables were all prepared and the pudding was boiling and making clouds of steam. In the front parlour, the tall Christmas tree was covered with tiny candles that would be lit at tea-time and under the tree were piles of presents all tied with string. The two sisters were both wearing new, similar and very becoming dresses. Everything was on course. It was going to be a great New Year!

Chapter 8

The Curry Comb Affair

At least three times a week, travellers of the commercial kind, came into the shop. Some of them had always worked in this line of business and knew how to make a living at it. These were the jolly, resilient men, usually Londoners, who often carried their own 'lines' and could turn even a slump into a time of commercial opportunity. Other sadder figures joined their ranks in the 1920's: former officers, businessmen whose investments had failed and members of the gentry who were victims of the stock market failure.

All of these men were greeted politely, if not always enthusiastically by both Tom and Nellie, Nellie offering cups of tea to the lesser known travellers whilst Tommy invited the old faithfuls into the cellar for a gargle, as he put it. Even if their wares were not required, Tommy would always try and place a minimum order to keep them going, for there was a very soft side to him which recognised that a man had a need for dignity and self-respect.

One cold March day however, things went differently. A thin, worn-out looking man came through the door clutching the usual commercial travellers' bag. He looked at the manager, as usual behind the bacon counter and hesitated, as if uncertain whether to go forward or beat a hasty retreat into the High Street. His luck changed however, because just as he was about to retreat towards the door Nellie finished with her customer and looking up she smiled.

"Can I help you? It's a dreadful day."

The traveller advanced, acknowledging her greeting and starting his sales pitch by introducing himself. He was interrupted by a voice that came angrily from behind the bacon counter.

"Short, his name is, Nellie, Short; Short by name, short on sense and short of money by the look of it."

The man turned as if stabbed.

"Badnell," he gasped, "Badnell."

"What have we got today then Shortie?" Tommy asked sarcastically. "A job lot of curry combs? Remember the curry combs eh, Shortie?"

His face was now so close to the poor grey man's head that it seemed he might be scratched with the prongs of the moustache as well as flecked with the spittle of anger and spite.

"And by the way, I'm Mr Badnell to you. Mr Badnell." He turned to the shop, "Don't look like a captain now, do he?"

He was reverting to Knowl Hill talk. This was the man who had put him on a charge in Italy for using a curry comb; how else were they to clean the poor wretched beasts? The army half killed the poor things and then expected him and his mates to clean them up and make them useable again. The only problem being that the officers had only ridden horses, they may have done a little light grooming, but they had never cleaned up plough horses or pack mules. They just made regulations and then put professional horsemen like him on charges when they went their own way in the face of stupid regulations.

"Know how I got to be manager?" He stuck his face right into the former officer's.

"I was the only one that could make the pony go. Anyone around here will tell you, me and horses go together." He turned with a sneer, "Tables are turned now eh, Shortie? You'd better get out. I always keep my own curry comb."

The traveller gave a lame look at Nellie and made for the door.

"Won't you have a cup of tea?" she called after him, "And thank you for calling."

He smiled at her kindness and she could see the sort of man he must have been in happier times. She came around the corner of the counter by the brass scales and caught up with the man just as he reached the fishmongers.

"I'm so sorry," she whispered and pressed half a crown into his hand and then turned away. Captain Short, as he had been, looked after the kind and beautiful woman. He pocketed the half crown, for he needed it and wondered how it was that such uncouth men as Private Badnell had the good fortune to have wives such as that.

When she got back to her position behind the biscuit counter only a few moments had passed.

"Where did you go?" asked her husband. Nellie smiled and answered with a white lie that he had left his pencil and she had returned it. So the morning ended. But Nellie was furious. As the door was closed for lunch and the blind pulled down she turned on him,

"How could you? How could you humiliate that poor man? I'm ashamed of you. How do you think you looked?"

She ran upstairs and made sure he didn't touch her when they washed their hands at the sink. Her eczema flared up and spread across her forehead.

"Why didn't you stay in Italy?" she hissed at him, "Stay with the mules and the peasants and the curry combs?"

She never seemed to see his point of view these days. Surely she could see that in the army that man had humiliated him? He tried to explain but all she would say was, "The war was over long ago. How could you Tom? Couldn't you see how ill he was? How could you?" and she moved into the living room and squeezed in between Ada and Kath.

"You can sit beside Dad today," she said.

She never sat beside him again if she could possibly help it.

Chapter 9

The Separation

Tommy lay awake. He had been awake for some time. He wanted to pull away the bolster, which separated him from his wife and put his arms around her. He did not. He often awoke and felt like putting his arms around his wife, but he did not. In the moments between waking, thinking and acting, he remembered what would happen if he did. Nellie would react with barely disguised disgust, endure what was clearly torture to her and she would then escape downstairs at the first opportunity. What was the point? There was no pleasure. He was simply left feeling wretched and unhappy; the act of marital union for Tommy and Nellie left both feeling separated and unfulfilled.

Tommy wondered how long this could go on. Quite a few women, he gathered from overhead conversations, were not eager for their husbands' attentions, but most seemed to accept that part of marriage as something that grownups did. At times it was good, at times indifferent and at other times a waste of time. But it was what married people did. It was no great feat of endurance, he was very normal in his likes. He had heard strange things when he was in Italy, of what men who went to brothels demanded, but even when he had come to believe the tales he heard, he could hardly believe them. Only the twisted minds of some of the officers he knew could think up such things he reflected. That was the trouble with the gentry; they had far too much time to think up such things. The working man, like himself, often hardly had the energy to do more than kiss his wife goodnight. Only people with others to do their work would have the inclination for such antics, disgusting as they were. The problem lay with Nellie. It had to be faced that she was frigid and he was not a man who was cut out to have a frigid wife, especially when only a few yards away his sister-in-law, his darling Ada, was sleeping in the back room. Ada was the sort of woman who knew what grownup people did and that it was normal, pleasurable and kept everyone happy, well almost everyone.

Tommy was a man who could always see a way around things. He was a firm believer that if you wanted something badly enough, there was always a way to get it. He glanced across at Nellie's sleeping back. She was such a pretty woman, why did the bolster have to be there? Would she have been like that with another man?

He began to think about one of the travellers who came in, a Mr Pilkington. Mr Pilkington was a successful traveller; he travelled for a prestigious company of wine merchants. He was prosperous and enjoyed his working life. Certainly he enjoyed talking to Nellie. Last Christmas he had given her a very nice set of fish knives and forks in a blue satin-lined box and as he had handed them over he had said, "Mrs Badnell, dear Mrs Badnell, this is a token of the esteem in which you are held by the company."

Then he had smiled one of those little smiles which men smile to women they like very much and hope to get to know a lot better.

Tommy had never been rude or offensive to Mr Pilkington. Not only was the man liked by all and known at Head Office, but he was also very large. One of those large, well-set men with grey eyes and fair hair who improve in middle age with a little extra weight and who seem universally popular, slow moving, easy going and jovial in nature. Tommy may well have felt able to bully the ill and shabby Captain Short, but pulling wry faces behind the back of the amiable Mr Pilkington was as far as he was prepared to go.

Tommy tried to imagine his wife in the embrace of the pleasant wine merchant, but try as he may, he could not imagine his wife relaxed in the embrace of anyone. When he had come back from the war, he had asked her if there had been anyone else but he had known the answer without asking. Nellie was at her happiest with her Dad, her sister and her children. Nellie should have been a nun.

Slowly a plan formulated in his head. Nellie did not want him and he did not want Nellie, but he did want Ada and at times Ada wanted him. He felt convinced that if Nellie were removed from the scene, he and Ada would be happy. As it was, Kathleen spent most of her time with 'Auntie' and Phil was now involved with the scouts, building his radios and tinkering with engines.

Tom thought for what seemed like hours on how he could, without bringing disgrace upon himself and the family, get rid of his wife, at least for a few weeks, so that he could have some time with her sister. There were several options, he could suggest that she move to her father's house, he could move her to one of his other houses, or she could move right away. The last option seemed the most attractive. An idea struck him. Kathleen had been ill with whooping cough. A little sea air would do them both good. That was it, they should go to the sea, and Brighton was very nice. Brighton was where they should go and leave him alone with Ada, he thought. There would be no bolsters with his sister-in-law of that he was certain.

The next time that Tommy found himself alone with Nellie, he decided to bring up the subject. They were very rarely alone, unless in bed, and somehow that did not seem a suitable place to discuss the subject of what was, in reality, their separation. He had no idea of how his wife would react. One of the problems of their marriage was that neither of them had any idea of what the other really felt. Nellie had told him that she had tolerated his physical demands in the early stages of their marriage because she knew that that was what was expected of her, but after the arrival of Kathleen she had shown that she found that side of their union both onerous and unpleasant. Maybe she would welcome the suggestion that they have, at the very least, a break from one another.

He could be generous, he could afford for them to stay in a nice place. Brighton in the winter should be full of nice empty hotels. He would allow Nellie four pounds a week - that should keep Kathleen and her in comfort. By the time he came to put things into practice however, his generosity had lessened. He remembered that he only officially gave Ada a pound a week to feed them all, so why should he give Nellie, the cause of all the trouble to his way of thinking, such a generous allowance just to swan around in Brighton.

"Nellie," he said in the rather wheedling way he had when he wanted something but knew he was in the wrong, "Nellie, I can't help noticing that young Kathleen is still coughing a bit and you don't look too bright yourself."

If the unexpected concern over the health of their daughter, who was no favourite of her father, caused Nellie considerable surprise, her husband's concern for her own health caused what amounted to nothing less than shock. Certainly it aroused in Nellie a sense of unease. She knew only too well Tom's ability to get whatever he wanted by fair means or foul. He was planning something, something which was not in her best interests or those of their daughter. She had not long to wait to find out more of his intentions, for as usual he overplayed his hand.

Nellie did not have her husband's scheming nature, but she had a strong sense of intuition. Regrettably, her sweet and soft nature rarely allowed her to make use of her own knowledge of human nature or to defend her own interests, but occasionally, when those she loved - such as her father or her children - were in danger of being wronged, she could stick up for herself and outwit her husband.

"I thought it might be an idea to take Kath to the seaside, to Brighton. Do you both good."

Nellie reminded him that Kathleen, along with Ada and Mona, had, in fact, had quite a long break in Margate, breathing in the fumes from the seaweed and that Kathleen was regularly taken round to the gasworks to breathe in the fumes as they were also said to be beneficial. When she looked at his face however, she could see that Kathleen's health was not what this was about. He wanted to get rid of them both. He wanted to be left alone with Ada and Phil. She knew that something similar to this had happened to other women: she knew of a woman in the town who had lost the shop which she had inherited, to a husband who had wanted to be rid of her.

Nellie thought quickly. She may have been a poor card player, but she had more patience than her husband so she smiled and asked, "And how long do you think we should stay?"

Tommy's patience was beginning to wear a little thin and he shot back at her, "As long as you like, as long as you like my dear."

Nellie's suspicions were confirmed and she alleged in a small voice, "You want to get rid of me don't you? You want to be rid of me and Kath so that you can live with Ada. That's it, isn't it?"

In the face of the truth, Tommy just looked at the table. Involuntarily he twisted his heavy gold wedding band and made a grunt of assent barely recognisable as, "Yes."

"Well, you've got it all worked out but you'll never get away with it. How do you think Mr Kilby will think? What about the assistants and the customers? How do you think you are going to fool all of them?" And finally, "I should think your chances of becoming mayor are just about over."

But Tommy knew that Nellie would never show him up. She could have stayed on as manager after the war and had him demoted to assistant manager had she wanted to, but the appearance of a solid, Christian and loving family had always been Nellie's prime concern. For this reason, she went along with all the lies and deceit. In her eyes, family respectability was the only thing that mattered and she was prepared to make any personal sacrifice to preserve it. Tommy's knowledge of this was his trump card. It would, at the very least give him a few delicious weeks with Ada, a few weeks of passion without all the scheming and hiding which accompanied most of their rare and brief liaisons.

Just as Tommy had thought, another family lie was spread with the assent, if not assistance, of his wife. She would, Nellie said, be taking Kathleen to Brighton for the good of her health. As with the matter of giving a home to his sister-in-law, Tommy managed to gain favour from this new development by assuring all and sundry that he had assured his dear wife that he could cope in the shop without her help.

Most of the assistants accepted the story without question but on Mr Pilkington's next visit, Nellie whispered, "I may not be here next time you call, Mr Pilkington. Mr Badnell is sending Kathleen and myself away to the sea for a bit, for our health you know."

Mr Pilkington turned and remarked to the manager that Brighton could be very cold indeed in March and perhaps it would be wisest to wait until May, or April at the very least. He also felt that the attractive Mrs Badnell did not look too enthusiastic about her forthcoming trip.

He well remembered the days in the war. Goodness me, she was a dazzler then. She ran that shop superbly, better in fact than her husband. She had always seemed so happy then, full of her trips out, going shopping in London, going to the tennis matches. Lately, although she smiled a lot, it was not the same smile.

49

He was very fond of Mrs Pilkington, an excellent woman who satisfied his every need, but he had often thought that had Mrs Pilkington not been there, he might well have entertained thoughts of the grocer's wife which were not entirely to do with business.

One unexpected difficulty arose when Tommy had said to his daughter, "How would you like to go to the seaside with your mum?" Her immediate reaction had been, "Is Auntie coming?" and she showed considerable distress at being separated from her aunt until the day of departure.

This answer was not what Tommy had wanted and caused poor Nellie even more pain than she was feeling already. She was in the process of being betrayed by her husband, she felt betrayed by the sister she loved and had loved all of her life and now even her daughter only wanted to be with her auntie. Nellie felt she would always be second best. She couldn't understand why God had punished her so. It seemed so unfair and try as she might, she could not remember a single bad thing that she had done. She always turned the other cheek, she said her prayers and she didn't drink. Nonetheless she was about to be put out in favour of her older sister who had arrived with two children, two fatherless children.

Nellie thought of her little niece Gladys. She had been so good, so lovely and yet she had been taken at such an early age. Perhaps she was lucky; a brief life full of love, a bright young death at nine years old and a glorious eternity surrounded by angels. Nellie was quite certain of that. Gladys would certainly be surrounded by angels. How she envied her niece at that moment of betrayal and misery.

Kathleen was placated with a box camera and a pair of fur gloves and on a cold and dreary day, Tom took his wife and daughter to the railway station and accompanied them to Paddington. In the taxi, he handed his wife a small brown envelope and said somewhat sheepishly, "That should keep you going for a couple of weeks and there is the address of the boarding house inside. It's all booked up; just give the address to the taxi man at the station."

Nellie had a natural dignity and pushed the envelope inside her handbag without counting the money but it did not feel a generous amount and practical anxieties begin to grow along with her feelings of rejection and isolation. Strangely, she felt no bitterness towards her sister, as she well might have done, for although she had welcomed in the husbandless Ada and her two children, she knew that Ada was not the architect of her sadness, it was Tom. He had proven to be as devious and cruel as his mother and brother. She thought of her parents, those two good people, she could almost hear her mother saying,

'There will always be someone with you Nellie. Lay your problems before the Lord.'

A small smile began to creep over Nellie's face. A sense of calm started to soothe the eczema and still her hands and she smiled at her daughter and said, "We are going to have a lovely time, aren't we Kath?" And the child, quite unexpectedly, put her arms around her mother's neck and said, "Yes, a lovely, lovely time."

Then she planted a rare but very welcome kiss on her mother's cheek. The two adults kept a sad and awkward silence, but the child chattered on about the sea, the pavilion and her camera and all the photos she was going to take to show auntie where they had been.

Tom bought the two tickets for Brighton and saw his wife and daughter onto the train but before the doors were finally slammed and the signal had been set for departure he gave them a token wave, turned on his heel and was off.

He was off to Ada, to all that he had hoped and planned for, all the warmth and passion that his wife failed to provide. With barely a thought for the wellbeing of Nellie and Kath, he reached Paddington, boarded the train for Maidenhead and within an hour he was walking down Queen Street with a light step, a song in his heart and a whistle on his lips. He was whistling, *'I'll be loving you. Always.'*

Ada was not at all sure about what was going on. Ada had gone through a great deal since she had left the family home in Merton. Along with all her brothers and sisters, Ada loved her parents very much, her father in particular. No matter what problems befell the Gardner family, her dear old Dad came smiling through. He was devoted to their mother and when neighbours made fun of his wife's gentility, he demonstrated in every way he could, how proud he was of her. Like him, Eliza had the highest of moral standards and he respected her greatly for this. Eliza came from gentry; she was a Hitcham, a family of trawler owners from Suffolk. When she had married Samuel, his elder brother, she had been cut off by her family. They strongly disapproved of her marrying a young man with no skills who worked in a dangerous occupation in the powder mills and worst of all whose mother ran an ale house. None of them had attended the wedding and Walter knew how much sorrow this had caused but as Louisa had said at that time and repeated to both her girls,

'If you find a man you love, then you must marry him. It is the only moral thing to do.'

Ada had wanted so often to return home but the thought of her dear parents' disappointment and sorrow made her stay away and although she had not known it then, her absence caused more heartache and sadness than any displeasure at her predicament could have done. She had wanted to explain to them that she had found a man she loved and he had loved her, but he had not had the strength her mother had had. In the end, he had married as his family advised and she had been left …

Tom had offered her security. He had also offered her affection and passion and now her little sister, little Nellie was in Brighton and she was here, in Nellie's place. Tonight she knew he would want her to share his bed, Nellie's and his bed. Ada sat at the big desk with a heavy heart. It just was not right. Poor Nellie and little Kath, he had not told her that Kath was to go too, but how could anyone, even Tom, separate a woman from her own daughter?

Ada was not a woman to shirk her domestic duties. Her very existence and those of her children had so often depended upon her excellent housekeeping ability, but today she could not get going. She was filled with a paralysing mixture of guilt, loss and foreboding. Ada was not religious in the way that her sister was and certainly not in the way of the dreaded old mother-in-law, rather she felt as a deer might – running towards what it knew would be a dead end, a trap, a path of no return. She looked up at the clock. It was five o'clock. Usually by now the fire would be roaring, the tea set, everything ready for the end of the day's business and the start of the evening. Nothing was done. She had sat there for hours gripped by indecision and dread. It was only the sound of Tom opening the door that finally roused her from the depressive grip which had held her since early morning.

She knew that Tom would be expecting to come home to a warm and amorous welcome, to a bright fire and his usual tea at the very least. She knew he would be disappointed, perhaps even angry, but there was nothing she could do. She had not thought once, in a loving way, about him all day. Her only thought was for her little sister, for Nellie, the small frightened girl she had held in her arms when they were small children and Nellie had been scared of the dark and the thunder. And Kathleen, how would Kathleen be doing? She was so used to having her there to tuck her in, so used to having her creep into the same room to sleep each night.

Ada's concerns were as they always were, for her sister and her niece. Yes, she had often enjoyed what Tom and she did to each other when the opportunity arose, but she had loved her sister and her niece all of their lives and their banishment from their own home disgusted her.

The sight of her brother-in-law, standing in the doorway holding a bunch of flowers seemed ridiculous and incongruous. He opened his arms and said, "Oh Ada, Ada, I love you so much." He kissed her as he did the first time they embraced in the railway carriage and drew her down onto his knee in the big Parker Knoll chair.

"Ada, I have waited so long for this, to have you to myself."

He drew her to him and for a short while Ada forgot her sister and niece, for like Tommy, she was quickly aroused and since Sergeant Derby there had been little passion in her life.

But in the early hours of the morning, Ada awoke. She was certain she could hear Kathleen calling, calling from Brighton, miles away from her own home where she belonged. Calling from Brighton where she had been sent so that her Auntie Ada could share her father's bed without interruption and whilst Tommy snored contentedly, Ada did what she had not done for many years, buried her head in the pillow and tried to muffle the sounds of her tears.

It was not only in the flat above the shop that things were not going as planned. Tommy had overlooked the fact that his wife was extremely important to other people if not to him and the more perceptive people with whom they mixed were puzzled, if not suspicious. Mrs James who always knew her sister's and niece's every move, appeared not to know the date of their expected return and on being questioned at which hotel his wife and child were residing, even the grocer appeared to have totally forgotten the name or road where they were staying.

After a week or so, Tommy realised that this could not go on. Downstairs he was constantly questioned about the health and welfare of his dear wife and delightful daughter and upstairs he was met, not with passion and affection but with a face torn with anxiety and guilt. Often, he could see that Ada had been crying. It was no good, he would have to fetch them back. It would be better to face the bolster than have that wretched Pilkington looking at him in a suspicious way and the girls were completely out of hand in the shop: orders were going amiss and the counters were not as tidy as when Nellie was there. He would put it off as long as he could, but there it was. They would just have to make the best of it for it now seemed as if Ada and Nellie and he were condemned to live together for the rest of their lives.

The next Saturday, Tom rose early. He left a note on the mantelpiece saying that he had urgent and important business and asked that Mr Hill act as Manager for the day. He put on his Homburg hat and before any of the other shops were open, walked up the High Street and then turning left into Queen Street made his way to the station. The clock in the tower at the entrance to the station approach showed just seven thirty. He should be in Brighton by lunchtime and with any luck they would be home by evening. Certainly, by the time the shop opened on Monday morning things would be back to normal.

Normal, fine and dandy.

Chapter 10

Brighton

Had Ada known the circumstances in which her niece and sister found themselves, she would not have hesitated in rushing down to Brighton herself to bring them both home. At the start of his plan to send his wife away, Tommy had intended his wife to go alone for although he thought Kathleen a stuck up little madam at times, she was his daughter and Ada was very, very fond of her. But when he had even hinted that Kathleen might stay, Nellie had reminded him that they were going to the sea for the good of Kathleen's health. Was that not what he had said? In any case, although Tommy wanted to be rid of his wife he knew even as he wronged her that what he was doing was unfair and unjust. How could he part from her from her child?

There was no way he could drive her out without her daughter. He was less understanding about her financial provision however. He had originally intended to allow her four pounds a week but when he placed the notes in the envelope, he had only given her four pounds to last for the two weeks until he visited them or sent further funds.

Nellie had always known how mean and cruel her in-laws could be. She had dreadful suspicions about the way her brother-in-law had treated his first wife – and she had suffered – almost died because of her treatment by Tom's mother. But she had never thought of Tom as cruel. Underhand, manipulative and mean, unfaithful and bullying certainly; but not cruel. On the journey to Brighton she realised that he could be very, very cruel, in the peasant-like, tight-fisted way his mother and brother were. He had given her half as much money as he had promised and the address to give the taxi driver was not a hotel as he had promised, it was a boarding house.

Nellie's heart sank. She felt that she had reached lower than she could ever reach. Rejected by both husband and sister and sent into exile in a shabby boarding house. But being Nellie she managed to smile for the child's sake, even though Kathleen's' contributions to the conversation consisted largely of how nice it would have been if Auntie could have come too and what should they take her home as a present?

Despite her low state, almost out of habit, Nellie rose to look in the mirror when she sensed that the train was pulling into Brighton station. She fastened the Astrakhan collar of her coat and straightened her matching hat, tucking a few wisps of dark brown hair beneath it. When the train had stopped, she fastened her daughter's coat, reminding her to put on her new fur gloves, and got down onto the platform to summon a porter. A porter was easily found. A lady in a long, fur-trimmed coat and matching hat accompanied by a small girl, also well dressed and with new fur gloves, soon attracted a burly man who accompanied them to the taxi rank. It was a long time since Nellie had had to think carefully about money, there had always been more than enough for their needs and whilst she lived with Tom, as his wife, he had never questioned any expenditure; she had always had whatever she wished. So his sudden unnecessary meanness was particularly hurtful. It was as if he wanted to emphasise that she was no longer his wife, no longer his partner.

Even Kathleen could not help but be aware that the taxi driver looked a little surprised when her mother handed over the slip of paper with the address of the boarding house. As he had seen them approach, he was sure that he would be heading to one of the pleasant hotels just off the front. The lady had nice clothes and luggage, so did the little girl. Ah well, he could usually guess a destination accurately but on this occasion he was so wrong. He repeated the address several times and then because he knew what a shabby place he was driving to, he would not even have recommended it to a commercial traveller, he venture, "There are some very nice places you know Madam. I could easily find you very pleasant and very cheap accommodation at this time of year."

The lady declined saying that the booking had been made and the accommodation recommended to her. But seeing the look of horror on both their faces when he drew up outside the run-down digs in the dingy back street, the taxi driver repeated his offer.

"On no, my husband would not know where to find us if we moved," said the lady.

"Your husband knows where you are staying?" persisted the driver.

He was certain he would never put his wife in a place like this. But he took his fare and realising that there was no chance of a tip, he drove away wondering what story lay behind a classy lady and the little girl booking into a place used by some pretty desperate people. Still, he thought, Brighton was full of such stories and that all helped to make his job interesting. He would put the riddle to his wife that evening and see if she had an answer. It was an enjoyable way of passing the evening and gave his wife a glimpse of what his job involved whilst he was away from her all day…

Nellie's training in the upper echelons of domestic service had given her very high standards. She well remembered the old housekeeper who had trained her saying that an experienced mistress would know how good her staff was the moment she set foot in a house, by the smell of the place. There are some scents which are welcoming and beneficial, said the ruler of the household: lavender in the bedroom is relaxing and pleasant, the scent of pine logs burning is welcoming to gentlemen, but there are some smells which must never be allowed in a house. The worst smell of all, totally unforgivable, is the smell of boiled cabbage. There is only one thing worse, she had emphasised to her new and impressionable trainee and that is cabbage that has burnt.

Even before she had opened the front door to the dark hall, Nellie recalled those words of wisdom; for here in this run-down, dingy and neglected hovel, resided all of the housekeeper's worst nightmares. The smell of cabbage, both boiled and burnt almost managed to smother the smell of old, stale cigar and cigarette smoke and yet, although the windows and doors were clearly never flung open each morning (first rule for any housekeeper or parlour-maid) the place was freezing cold. It was the sort of cold that made you know that the house had never been warm. The whole building was like a corpse, the corpse of a tramp; someone who had lain down out of sheer exhaustion and boredom. It was rotting, it was cold, fetid and unloved, and no wonder, for nothing in its location, its furnishings nor its design prompted anything but feelings of contempt and loathing.

There was a long pause before either new arrival said anything, but just as Kathleen had started to ask, "We are not staying here are we Mum?"

A bead curtain at the end of the passage parted and a person, totally at one with the establishment, advanced towards them, smiling a smile that did little but betray the urgent need for dental attention.

"Mrs Badnell," she drawled, "and Kathleen, isn't it? I've heard so much about you."

She said this to her two new guests as if the information might prove to be reassuring.

"Who told you? Who told you about us?" Asked Kathleen, and in the direct way of nine year olds, "I'm sure none of our friends would have stayed here. If they had, they would have told me about it ..."

She was about to say that they would have told her about the smell of cabbage and the dirty furniture but she was interrupted by the landlady, that is who she was, smiling and saying in a coy and meaningful way, "It was your Daddy, it was your Daddy told me all about you," she emphasised the *all* and turning to Nellie continued.

"Didn't old Tommy tell you that I got to know him at the races? He said he was looking for somewhere for his wife," she paused here and gave Nellie an unwelcome little smile, "and his little girl to come and stay. I said I'd give him very good rates as it was for a long let."

The amount of insight into her dire situation which Nellie gained from this sugared innuendo, made her feel genuinely faint and in a stiff and formal voice, she asked for them to be shown to their room. A little voice inside her kept saying, *'You are Helen Badnell. You own a house. You are respectable. You have influential friends. This cannot go on.'* But another voice said that other women had been treated far worse and oh yes, it could go on and unless she could be strong, brave and resourceful, it almost certainly would.

The next two weeks passed by slowly. The weather was cold but it was still better out of the digs that in them. Had there been more money, Nellie could have taken Kathleen out to tea or they could have gone shopping. As it was, whilst they were walking through the Lanes, Kathleen spied a fire screen. It was in the shape of an oriental girl, kneeling and holding up a parasol which formed the major part of the screen. Normally, Nellie would have haggled with the man a little then given her daughter the cash to pay for it. But on this occasion, she was unable to do so. One of the worst aspects of their time in Brighton was Kathleen's insistence each day that they go and look at the fire screen for Auntie. It seemed that everyone loved Ada. Would anyone ever think of her in so kindly a way?

The food in the digs was so inedible that most of the two pounds had gone by the end of the first week. Nellie had no desire to see Tom. She did not want to see his bald head, his spiky moustache nor his co-respondent shoes again. But she did want to go home. She wanted to see her son, the customers and assistants and strangely she also wanted to see Ada. Somehow she knew that this was not of Ada's doing. It was Tom and perhaps she was a little to blame also, but she just hated it so. When she had confided to her aunt, she had just said, *'oh shut your eyes and think of England.'* But Nellie could not. There were so many disgusting things in the world!

Towards the end of the second week, the money was running dangerously low and when Kathleen had asked once again when they could buy the going home present for Auntie, Nellie had come near to snapping at her daughter. She understood that buying presents had always been an integral part of family holidays, but this was NOT a holiday. It was a punishment and banishment. Kathleen could not understand this, but she did.

Nellie looked down at her daughter's face. She could not explain that she had almost no money left, that very soon, not only would they be unable to buy Auntie a present to take home, they would also be unable to take shelter in a tea shop or café. Then she remembered, she could hear his jeering voice, when she had once been stranded without money before, when she had ridden her bicycle all the way to Wimbledon to see her dear Dad and had a puncture on the way home.

'Well you stupid woman, you could have left your wedding ring at the bike shop until you went back with the money,' he had said. But the idea of removing her wedding ring was something Nellie had never contemplated, until now. What was the point of a wedding band if there was no marriage? And at that moment her bond with her small, eager daughter, looking up expectantly, was of far more importance to her than the wretched man who had placed her in this impossible predicament.   Nellie was not a naturally angry or

indignant person, but it was not only she but her child who was being badly treated and all of her maternal protective love went into action.

"You go and look in the window and see if the fire-screen is still there," she urged, "I am just going to the bank to get some money."

She left Kathleen looking in the window of the shop at all the Crest china and the models made of shells. She had seen a pawnbroker's shop up the road and taking her wedding ring from her finger she went confidently into the shop. She was, after all, she reminded herself, a respectable woman brought by some terrible trick of fate to this sorry state of affairs.

"I want to sell this wedding ring," she blurted to the man behind the counter.

"You could pawn it," offered the man kindly, "that way you could come back and get it when you have the money."

"No," affirmed Nellie, "I wish to sell it. I shan't be coming back."

She didn't haggle on the price. It was more than enough to buy the fire-screen and have money over for several visits to the tea shop. By the time the money ran out, Nellie had decided she would have found a solution. She would write to Mr Kilby. She could and would fight back, if not for her, for Kathleen and Phil. What on earth had Tom told their son she wondered? Kath skipped ahead, chattering away and asking when she could go home as her cough was now cleared up and she ought to go back to school.

When they returned from their walk, bracing themselves for the smell which was about to hit them, a falsely cheerful voice greeted them with, "Who's got a nice surprise then? Whose Daddy's come to see them?"

Nellie looked down and the first thing she saw was her husband's brown and white co-respondent shoes. She was reluctant to look up at his face, but when she did, it was not the face that she had expected to see. It was looking down at the hat he was turning between his hands and he confessed, "Ada thought I ought to come and see if you're alright. She's worried about you. I am too," he added, "worried; came to see if Kathleen is alright. Ada says she shouldn't be missing so much school."

"And what did Ada say about me? Is she worried about me, or does she just want my daughter? She has my home, my husband and now my daughter."

She sensed the beads moving at the end of the dark tunnel of the hallway and added, "And I'm to be left with a trollop from the racecourse, in a filthy doss house. Either I go back with you today Tom, back to my own home and children or I will write to Mr Kilby."

He started to interrupt her but the small assertive voice which she had started to hear in her darkest hours insisted, "I don't want to Tom, but if you make me, I can make life very difficult for you."

She was surprising herself. Usually she could never stand up to anyone, certainly not Tom, but faced with losing everything, in particular her children, she found a new, almost desperate cunning and anger. She still did not want to tell him about the house in Fielding Road, she wanted to keep that secret, that trump card. Somehow Tommy knew that there was something he was not aware of, something he should treat with caution. There was silence for quite a while, broken only by the rattle of beads and then a common voice drawled,

"Everything alright then? Nice cup of tea, Tommy?"

"I'll be taking my wife and daughter home today," he retorted, and reading her rapidly hardening expression.

"Yes, I know I said a long let but we've changed our minds. I think we shall have our tea in the town."

The small family walked down to the promenade and apart from an unfortunate incident involving Kathleen taking a photo of her father, at his insistence, and losing one of her fur gloves in the process, they looked like any other family group. True, the mother had style and even chic and the father looked a little flashy and hard, but as they walked through the Lanes to purchase the oriental fire-screen from the antique shop, no-one would have guessed that their marriage had come to within a whisker of collapse. And none of them would ever have guessed that just as they were purchasing her gift, Ada was awaiting their return with excited, if apprehensive anticipation. For Kathleen and Nellie, if not for Tom, she had prepared well; the furniture shone, the fire leapt and the cake in the oven smelled wonderful. When she had sent Tom to fetch back Kathleen, she knew that Nellie would come back too. She was so glad. Whenever she had been away from her sister, things had gone wrong – for both of them. She had no idea how they were ever going to resolve things, but she did know that none of them would ever be happy apart.

Chapter 11

Nellie and the Mynah Bird

Nellie's nerves were worsening. Everyone around her could tell the accumulation of the stresses in her life were becoming insupportable. The nightly torment of sharing a bed with a man she was coming more and more to loathe meant that she rarely slept unless she took pills. With increasing frequency, she visited the doctor for prescriptions and being an astute and kindly man, he knew he could only ease the most obvious symptoms of her distress. So he gave her the drugs she needed in order for her to have a minimal amount of sleep. Dr Simons knew however, that sooner or later the combination of soothing and sleeping pills he prescribed would be of no use. He knew that the living arrangements in the flat above the grocery store were cramped and also irregular and that this was at the cause of his patient's unhappiness.

He could never understand how some couples had ever come to be couples, so unsuited did they seem, and the combination of the soft and refined Mrs Badnell with her bossy and really rather vulgar husband were just such a case in point. He had no idea how he could help the lady in the long term. It was her husband who was the root of the problem. Her health had been excellent when he was away at the war. Certainly, she cited her husband's snoring as the major cause of her insomnia and undoubtedly, this combined with also having to work all day in the company of the man brought her to a state of perpetual and heightened stress. The eczema which at one time simply appeared as a small red mark above her left eyebrow in times of agitation was now a permanent fixture and occasionally it seemed to spread, like a strawberry mark, across the whole of her upper face.

The town's doctor was not the only one concerned about Nellie's health. Ada also worried about her sister. Despite the nature of their domestic arrangements and the fact that in the early stages there had been times of coolness and resentment between them, Ada and Nellie loved one another deeply. Ada knew that the situation was impossible for them all, but mainly for Nellie. They were not poor, as people went, by the standards of the day they were very well off; but although she and Nellie had worked towards the wealth of the family, in the shop, collecting the rents (and there were a lot of those now) Tom of course held all the money. He relied upon their hard work, their honesty and their thoroughness but it was he who went to see the Bank Manager, he who signed the cheques. Things had to change. The money had to be more evenly spread. The way things were, Tom could put them all out onto the street and no-one could stop him.

Nellie, everyone agreed, had the very sweetest of natures. All that she had learnt from her God-fearing parents and from the officers at the Salvation Army had taken root in the fertile tilth of her young mind and had anchored there with strong and binding ties. Nellie really believed that all humans should do unto others as they would be done by and that turning the other cheek was the best way to avoid confrontation. Until her marriage, the only unkind thing that Nellie could ever remember doing was throwing mud over the step of a woman who had refused to pay her for cleaning it. Much to Nellie's amazement she had managed to get away with that and she realised that had she wanted, she could have got away with an awful lot more. No-one ever suspected that sweet face of wickedness or spite, but after her treatment at Tom's hands and the banishment to Brighton, Nellie felt a little core of spite and anger sometimes. It had nothing to do with her sister, or her daughter, but a great deal to do with Tom. Nellie could have gone to Mr Kilby of course, she could have leaked the news of her shameful treatment around the town, but then the family honour would have been tarnished, Ada would have been branded as an adulteress and life for Kath and Phil would have been appalling. Tom, strangely enough, would be the one to come out of it best of all. That was how things worked! The men got off scot free and the women carried the shame and blame. Nellie had no intention of losing her place in society and certainly no intention of jeopardising her children's situation. Nellie went back to smiling and turning the other cheek. She genuinely showed her sweet nature to the customers and the nicer class of traveller like Mr Pilkington, but the grocer's legal wife watched her husband behind the bacon counter and thought that one day she would make him suffer too. She would never be able to match the hurt and humiliation that she had suffered, but suffer he would. She just had to wait for the right time and an opportunity would arise.

As if the guardian angel of wronged wives was looking after Nellie personally, the right opportunity did arise soon after. Tom had a way with animals, he loved them. He particularly loved birds, although as Nellie often reflected his love did not extend to him compelling her to force feed the geese in the darkened shed at Canesaro.

One day, during the time of the fair which was held on the moor near to the river, Tom came into the shop beaming, "Look what I have got, Nellie, come and see," and with that he whisked a bright red and gold cloth off a very large cage and there stood a large bird, one Nellie had never seen before.

"It's a mynah bird," he beamed, "you can teach them to talk. Look," he continued, "I'll have it talking in no time."

He went to the back of the shop and handed the bird a raisin he had picked from out of an opened sack.

"Who's a pretty girl then?" he asked pursing up his lips, "who's a pretty girl?"

The bird replied with a ghastly croaky caw-caw sound which appeared to entrance her new owner.

"Who's a very pretty girl then?" and again the rasping sound filled the shop. The sound reminded Nellie of something or someone and when she realised that it was the harridan who had been her tormentor in Brighton, the fate of the poor mynah bird was sealed.

Of course Nellie couldn't just kill the bird. She had no idea how to. In any case, she wanted Tom to get fond of the wretched thing and learn what it is like to lose something you love. So she waited. Tom certainly knew how to teach the bird. Very soon it was screeching, "Tommy, Tommy, Who's a pretty girl?"

The customers were fascinated, so were the assistants – the favoured ones like Doreen were allowed to offer raisins and small pieces of carrot.

One day, one of the errand boys picked up a small piece of bacon and was about to push it through the bars of the cage when Tom intervened immediately, "Never, ever give a bird anything with salt.

You'll kill it stone dead," he told the startled boy, "Never give that bird anything unless I tell you."

Nellie remembered the incident. She did recall from feeding the geese something about no salt, so she smiled at the lad and said, "You weren't to know. No harm done I am sure. Who would have thought it, that salt will kill a bird? Well fancy that!"

Nellie tucked the information away in her mind. She now knew the means; she had only to wait for the right time.

The right time was to arrive on the day that Ada went to the butchers and informed him that the family felt like a change.

"We seem to have the same thing week in and week out," she announced, "Joint, chops, mince, liver and bacon."

"You certainly keep a good table for them all, Mrs James," replied the butcher. "How about a nice piece of salt beef? Very tasty. Just serve it up with some carrots and potatoes - a veritable feast!"

He produced a fine piece of beef, ample for the five of them and a little left over for a sandwich. Unwittingly, Ada carried home the means of Nellie's revenge. The meat was set to simmer on the old gas stove with some root vegetables whilst Ada completed the rest of her many tasks. The new addition to the weekly menu was approved by all, Tom in particular. He always enjoyed his food, particularly if it was savoury and robust.

"Very nice, Ada, very nice, tasty, you can cook that again."

Nellie joined in the consensus that the salt beef should become a regular meal. She could bide her time, there would be future opportunities.

The bird became quite a celebrity. Tom certainly had a way with it. He would smilingly put his pursed lips to the cage and coo,

"Who's a pretty girl? Who loves old Tommy?" and the bird would shriek, "Tommy, Tommy, Tommy," to the delight of the assistants and customers. Nellie smiled as she always did but she hated the shrieking, nasty creature. Every time it squawked, she remembered the bead curtains in Brighton and the beak-faced harridan who had known far more about her embarrassing position than she would have wished.

Time passed. At one point, Nellie thought that she would maybe get used to the creature and not carry out her plan. It was, after all, only a bird – a defenceless creature that had never really harmed her.

Then, one afternoon Tommy opened the door of the cage and the bird hopped out onto his hand. He stroked the top of its head with his finger and cooed to it in a way that he had never cooed to her, or his children.

"Come here, Nellie, quietly." He was almost cooing at her. He beckoned to her with his other hand. "Don't be afraid, just stroke the top of her head – softly now. She's still nervous, but she's coming on so well, aren't you my lovely?"

Nellie reached out her hand; she was actually quite enthralled, quite amazed at the sheen on the bird's plumage, it's small bright eyes looking at her. As Tom moved his soothing finger from the bird's head, Nellie lifted her finger and in a trice, before either Tom or Nellie could stop it, the bird had grasped Nellie's finger and delivered a deep and painful gash. Nellie screamed in panic and in no time, Tom had bundled the bird back into the cage.

"Get the iodine straight away. Nellie has been hurt."

He said nothing to the bird who sat silently and malevolently staring at her victim but after he had covered the cage with its gaudy cloth, he turned to Nellie and said, "I didn't know you didn't like her. They always know. It's funny, but they always do. She knows you hate her, I can tell."

Nellie brushed it off.

"I must have moved suddenly," she explained, "Why should I hate the bird?"

She turned and went up the stairs holding her painful hand and knowing that the bird had to go and the bird behind its red and gold curtain knew that one day, the creature who seemed so kind and gentle would kill her even though Tommy, who she loved so much, would try to save her.

Chapter 12

Phil

Nellie had wondered in Brighton just what tale Tom and Ada had spun to explain to Phil the absence of his mother and sister. Phil was now seventeen and it was hard to fob him off with some daft story about his sister's health. His mum had looked very sad as she waved goodbye, even sadder than usual and Kathleen kept saying she was quite well, she had been to Margate with Auntie and made to smell the seaweed. It was only his Dad who seemed enthused with the prospect of them having a break in Brighton.

Phil was nearly a man. He thought in four or five years' time he would be getting married. He spent a lot of time with the scouts and whilst they were away at camp and away from the prying ears of their parents, the boys chatted and swapped information so that by the time they were seventeen and walking out with girls, they had a fair idea of what was what and what men and women did once the bedroom door was closed. Phil knew things were not as they should be between his dear mum and dad and after one day when he was sent home from school, he knew why.

It just so happened that it was a Thursday when he had fallen in the playground. Everyone knew it was early closing day and so the games master reasoned someone would be able to look after the boy, take him to the doctors if needed. Thursday was the day Nellie went round to see her dad at the White Cottage, Ada caught up with the paperwork and his Dad went down into the cellar, his own private domain, to plan the next BTR Dance, the old time dances he had revived and which were now so popular that they ran twice monthly.

Phil let himself in. His Dad was not in the cellar. He went up to the first small landing and called for Auntie. He felt quite poorly and would have liked her to look at his knee, but she was nowhere to be seen. They would never have gone out and left the door unlocked. He struggled up the next flight of stairs and flung himself on his bed, hugging his knee. Then, he heard it, a strange noise, coming from

Auntie's room next door. Phil couldn't make it out, a strange sound like a cat moaning to be let out. He tiptoed to the door and gently opened it a crack, just in case the cat should fly out. The first thing he saw was his father's bald head and beneath that, his aunt's face her mouth open and her eyes closed. Phil closed the door as quietly as he had opened it and stumbled down the stairs. He was only thirteen at the time and although he had some idea of what he had seen, he did not know how to react or what to do. He sat on a soda siphon crate in the yard gasping and waited until he had some idea of what he had seen. He did not know how to react or what to do. He said nothing but he never looked at or thought of his father or aunt in the same way again. When he was alone he cried, for his poor dear mum. It was then he decided that he knew who he would marry and like many of Phil's decisions, it was a very wise one.

So yes, he remembered that afternoon and Phil had a good idea why Kath and Mum had been sent away. He realised a few other people had guessed as well. He joined in the surly sulking mood of the assistants and rarely answered his Dad. Auntie seemed to cry a lot and he knew it was inevitable that soon Mum and Kath would be home. But Phil had seen a different sort of family life just up the High Street with the Pragnells and he hoped that one day, Olive would make a family with him. Olive was not a great beauty but whenever she looked at him, she smiled. That was what he wanted, more smiles. The thought made him smile too and he decided to get on with his life as soon as possible and leave his Dad to get on with his.

After that dreadful afternoon when he felt so betrayed, he had gone up the High Street to their friends the Pragnells. As usual Olive had come out and smiled at him and when he went to hold her hand, she didn't pull away.

"Olive", he asked, "When we are grown up, do you think we should get married?"

She smiled and he knew then where his future lay. For the next few years he could enjoy the scouts, Meccano, building radios and motorbikes and one day he hoped he would get an apprenticeship at Hewens the garage near to Lent Rise.

Yes Phil knew what it was all about but his future lay elsewhere and although he was sad for his Mum, he was not going to let their problems spoil his life. Cars, the scouts and Olive were his future.

If only he had known that Dunkirk, Africa and the army were also going to play a big part too. But for now he was content.

Chapter 13

Beulah

Nellie, Ada knew, had an ace up her sleeve; she had a house in her own right. It was something which she had instinctively kept from Tom, knowing that he would bitterly resent the independence which property ownership gave her. Also, the manner in which she had gained this asset and independence would anger him and cause problems between them and the owner of the shop, Mr Kilby.

Mr Kilby was a very shrewd and perceptive man. He had grown up under the shadow of his father's bankruptcy but he had discharged it in full, single-handedly. Once having scrimped and saved for years to achieve this feat of honour, parsimony had become a way of life to the gentleman and although he was generous in spirit, he was often reluctant to part with money. At the start of the Great War, he had been dreadfully concerned about his business interests. It was soon clear that all able-bodied men would be called up and that commerce would be left in the hands of the women.

At the start of the war, he watched his business interests more carefully than usual and soon discovered that Mrs Badnell seemed to possess more business acumen than her husband. Along with her sister, she ran the shop with charm, efficiency and humour. Even old Mr Hill looked happy and to his amazement, when young Mr Breed came back with the figures, the profits had leapt. Each quarter they got better. Mr Kilby wished that Mrs Badnell would manage the shop indefinitely. Of course, there had been the unfortunate matter of the ration coupons. The outcome of this had ultimately reflected well, not only on Mrs Badnell but also on the store. It had come about because of the dear woman's sympathetic nature, and of course the ministry's very stringent enforcement of food rationing. The ministry simply did not seem to understand what he and his staff did, how very difficult it was to refuse women butter when their sons or husbands were coming home from the front, or to refuse women sugar for jam making when the fruit was rotting in the basket or on the tree. There had been more food actually wasted thought Mr Kilby through the actions of politicians, than any other factor. When he met up with some of them, as he surely would, at the tennis in Wimbledon, he would make a point of telling them so.

Poor Mrs Badnell had been taken to court. Not only was her face almost covered by eczema but the doctor had to prescribe something to enable her to attend court. Her stomach had felt the full impact of the worry, distress and fear of prison and for days she could barely leave the small bathroom on the landing.

Nonetheless, when placed in the dock of the magistrate's court she made a very comely sight. The local magistrate, after hearing a mountain of evidence from loyal and grateful customers and also sensing the mood of the respectable, well-presented members of the public in the gallery, decided to discharge her.

He peered in a kindly way over the top of his spectacles and giving a sideways nod to Mr Kilby, who had come down in person for the trial, affirmed, "Your employer tells the court that you are a lady of the very highest moral and business standards and your customers have informed this court that the discrepancy incurred with the food rationing coupons came about due to your good nature. Alas, Mrs Badnell, war-time is no time for a sweet nature such as yours. I must therefore ask you to refrain from your usual kindness and good nature until hostilities have ceased. You may then go back to providing the populace of this town with their usual vast quantities of extremely high class groceries."

At this point he again nodded towards Mr Kilby. He continued, "I am sure we all join with you in hoping that Mr Badnell will soon return safely and relieve you of the strain of running the shop single-handedly."

Nellie stood in the dock feeling rather bewildered.

"You may go," clarified the magistrate, "there is no case to answer, but please, dear lady, try to be a little harder. There are always those who will take advantage of a soft and generous nature. You must be on your guard."

Mr Kilby was not the only man in the court that day who realised what a soft nature Nellie had, or how easy she was to take advantage of when she saw her old and valued customers struggling with the meagre rations. Mr Kilby had long suspected that the lady stepping down from the dock, in a most becoming hat (where did she get her hats he wondered) was not treated in the way she should be, not only by her husband, but also by his mother. No wonder women wanted the vote, he thought. This war had really shown the country what they could do and if a soft heart was their only drawback, then he was all for drawbacks. Customers liked kindliness and a gentle manner when they were shopping. He could foresee a time when shopping would be fun; people would look forward to going to the shops. He had read about developments in America. He had always believed that groceries could be exciting.

Now, with the case successfully over, and the crowd from the gallery gathering around Nellie to congratulate her, the owner of the shop had to make an important decision. He felt it was his contribution to women's rights, a contribution in his usual quiet but highly effective way. It had always been the custom to pay the managers a bonus after a particularly good year and the Maidenhead shop had three consecutive years with record profits. A bonus must be paid out; should it go to the absentee manager or his wife? Mr Kilby thought about it long and hard. He remembered all that his father had inflicted on his mother, her sadness and her shame. He decided he must do what was fair; he must give the very considerable bonus to the one who had earned it. She was very pretty, quite apart from her business acumen and he didn't like the way her husband spoke to her.

The next time the owner visited his shop, he asked to speak with Mrs Badnell. At first she was concerned and flustered, wondering if everything was in order, but she quickly relaxed when she saw his smile and heard his assurances of complete approval and satisfaction. He wanted this pleasant, hard-working and efficient little woman to have some security. He did not want her to be at the mercy of her husband who was likely to return from Italy at any time. He had made enquiries in the town; he had made a plan for the future safety and well-being of the pretty Mrs Badnell who had served the interest of his commercial enterprises so well throughout the war. She was a traditionally loyal wife however, and he had to tread carefully in order for her to agree to his plan. He explained that some new and pleasant properties were being built up the hill on the edge of the thicket. They were pleasant family homes and would make a good investment for when she and Tommy eventually retired. He was careful to include her husband but also pointed out that the rental income from the property would guarantee her standard of living when her husband returned and she was no longer paid the Manager's wage. All this made sense to Nellie. She and Mr Kilby went to view the house for sale in Fielding Road. Fielding Road. It had such a nice sound to it. She knew she had been cheated of her first home by that old witch of a mother-in-law. This would be her house, nothing to do with Tom; her promised land. She remembered the Bible classes at the Salvation Army and her dear old dad reading Pilgrims Progress. She would call it Beulah, the Promised Land.

She turned to her employer, "Thank you Mr Kilby," she beamed, "you have made me a very happy woman. I think it is an excellent idea to buy the house for our retirement and I think we should get the papers signed as soon as possible."

"So do I, my dear," agreed the old man, "your husband may be back next week and you will be far too busy then."

Nellie accompanied her employer to the solicitors around the corner. Stuchbery's would sort out the paperwork as quickly as possible and she could slip round at any time and sign the necessary papers.

Nellie could hardly believe this was happening. She had always wanted her own home, wanted a house near the country and suddenly, quite unexpectedly, she was getting just what she wanted. She thought how wonderful it would be to live there alone. She could grow flowers – roses, and each morning she would rise and polish the door step so that everyone knew what a particular woman lived there. Then she thought of the scandal. No respectable woman ever left her husband, no matter what he did. It was unfair but that is how it was. Women were still expected to keep the peace and do the appeasing and that is what she and Ada would continue to do. They had always managed to remain respectable so Tom must not know about the house. Luckily, he was a most unsuspicious man and left all of the day to day financial side of the family to her so it was unlikely that he would find out unless someone told him.

So Nellie had become a property owner through her own efforts. It was a long time before Tom found out. She knew he wouldn't like it. She was quite right.

Chapter 14

Gladys, The Little Angel

The passion between Tom and Ada had cooled with time but Ada's compassion for her sister was unchanging and meant that more and more she fell out with Tom. There would always be, for the rest of their lives, a certain feeling for one another, but they were now middle-aged and the children were having romances of their own. Ada had to think of the future: for herself, for Nellie and the girls. When she said the girls she meant Mona, her own daughter, and Kath. Phil, of course, would be provided for. He was the son and Tom did love him. Phil had been borne out of love. Tom had always had a strange way of showing his love for Nellie but in the early days he had loved her and been thrilled with the birth of their son. Phil had been sent to the grammar school and his father had willingly paid the fees. Kath however had been conceived much against his wife's wishes, in an attempt to keep him from the army, but to no avail. In his eyes this had been her first great failure.

Ada had suffered the sorrow of losing one of her daughters. The sweet and lovely Gladys had died aged nine quite tragically. Ada largely blamed Tom, although she herself was partly to blame. As with so much in the family they had produced a credible story which they had all kept to and everyone accepted. Nevertheless, within the family they all knew, deep down, that the desire for profit, the old Badnell peasant ways of throwing nothing away were to blame.

One of Tom's side-lines was pig keeping, it was highly profitable. You bought a young pig and fed it all the waste food, windfalls from the orchard at Canesaro and any old greengrocery that friend Bill was throwing out. Certainly Tom's pigs usually thrived on this method of feeding. Just before Gladys' tragic death, swine fever was discovered in the area. Government officials told everyone to slaughter their pigs and officials would come and remove the carcasses for burning. The thought of such waste put the whole family into a state of frustration. What did government officials know about pigs argued Tom? About as much as officers knew about grooming horses, he thought; but he didn't say this in front of Nellie. They all particularly loved fried pig's liver and bacon and Tommy decided to remove the pig's liver prior to the carcass being taken away. The large pig's liver was placed in the larder in preparation for tomorrow's lunch. Ada had some nice bacon and onions to go with it and perhaps they would have some runner beans at the green grocers. Gladys would love it, she was very partial to liver, it was her favourite.

That evening, when everyone else was out of the flat apart from Ada and her younger daughter, Gladys came down the stairs and wove her arms around her mother's neck. Ada loved all children. She had an affinity with them and her two daughters were particularly dear. She could refuse her nothing. Gladys was the one she had always kept with her. Nothing would ever persuade her to part with Gladys. So when the little girl asked her mother if she would cook her just a very little of the liver as she really couldn't wait for tomorrow lunchtime, Ada happily set to and cooked two slices. It smelled and looked delicious. She found some potatoes to fry with it and the little girl ate it with relish. I'm lucky she smiled to her mother as she turned at the door before going back to bed, I shall have my favourite meal twice in two days. Ada told her to be quiet about it as the others might be jealous.

Within an hour Ada heard the unmistakeable sounds of a child retching. She rushed to Gladys who was already delirious with fever. Ada screamed to the neighbours for help and Gladys was soon in the Cottage Hospital, but by midnight she was dead. The doctor said it must be peritonitis (Ada did not mention the liver) and it was agreed that the cause of death was a ruptured appendix. Even in the depths of her grief, Ada remembered to dispose of the liver in the butchers' bin at the back of the yard. No-one else in the family asked about it; they were all distraught. Gladys had been a beautiful little girl: happy, good and sweet-natured. Tom had loved her and found her an easy child to have around. The story in the town was that Gladys had been too good for this world and only the angels were fit to have her. The doctor however, had reason to doubt this theory but knowing what a greatly loved child she was, he never for one moment suspected ill treatment and thinking that the mother had suffered enough, he let the funeral proceed. The child was well nourished, clean and well cared for. There had never been any suspicion of appendicitis but in children these things sometimes flared up quickly and there was nothing he could do to save her. He almost thought it could be poisoning but it was not a poison with which he was familiar.

So little Gladys was placed beneath a kneeling angel and the matter was pushed to the back of people's minds. *'A little angel'* they would say and shake their heads. Although Ada hardly mentioned her child after her death, she never recovered from it and her love for Kathleen grew ever stronger, unwittingly driving a wedge between the girl and her own mother.

As was usual with the family, they presented a united and lasting front to the world, *'Gladys was too good for this world,'* they all said, *'only the angels were good enough to care for Gladys.'* In the end they came to believe what they told the town; the memory of the pig's liver was pushed to the back of their minds only to re-emerge in times of stress or in old age when the most uncomfortable thoughts tend to return unbidden. But at the time, only the doctor pondered on how a child could develop peritonitis so quickly. He was perfectly certain that she was one of the most loved and well cared for children that he had ever attended and he let the matter rest. She was also one of the most sweet-natured and beautiful children he had ever attended.

Maybe the old wives were right … Gladys James was an angel and Maidenhead had been lucky to share her for the few years that she was mortal.

Chapter 15

The Patient Mr Hill

Perhaps it was inevitable that sooner or later things would come to a head and perhaps it was not surprising that it was at Christmas time that the inevitable tragedy occurred. As usual, just before Christmas, there was even more work than ever. The errand boys came back with orders in the blue duplication books that ran to two pages and sometimes more.

Mr Hill, dear Mr Hill, who took so much of the brunt of Tommy's bossiness and sneering, worked away in the back of the shop making up orders in cardboard boxes all day, rarely stopping to stir a cup of tea with his pencil before drinking it and then soldiering on. Sometimes he was held up as not enough currants or demerara sugar had been weighed out and then he would have to judge whether to stop and weigh them out himself or get another assistant to do it. The last time he had stopped and weighed up some sultanas, Mr Badnell had come to the back of the shop and told him brusquely that the orders were needed to go out then and there. The errand boy was waiting, said the manager, he had not been told to weigh up - that was the younger assistant's jobs.

So, on this grey and damp day, just a few days before Christmas, Mr Hill noticed that the pile of weighed up raisins in the blue paper bags was running low and went through to the main shop to ask for a junior to help him. He saw Mr Badnell ahead of him, talking to a new and pretty girl called Doreen and asked if she might come to the back of the shop and weigh up half a sack or so of raisins because they were going fast. Each order it seemed, required at least a pound of them.

"Doubtless for the last minute puddings," volunteered the small, grey Mr Hill.

The young girl started to follow the elderly man to the back of the shop in response to the older woman's nod of approval but was cut short at the bacon counter by the Manager.

"Lost the use of your arms then Hill? What's the matter with you weighing up a few raisins? If you're getting too old and slow for the job you know what you can do." Then turning to the young girl, "Come with me Doreen, I need a hand wrapping the hams. We are all busy today, it's not just Hill and his orders that need a bit of help."

He guided the young girl through the narrow space to the bacon counter. She looked at Nellie and slightly lifted her shoulders in an expression of bewilderment. Mr Hill's shoulders did not lift. He trudged back to the rear of the shop and began to untie the sack, open the flattened bags and weigh up the raisins. Everyone knew that two people working on this job made it easier and quicker than only one. It was also more pleasant and it would have been nice with Doreen. She was a pleasant and kindly girl.

Soon afterwards, Mrs Badnell came through with a mug of tea.

"There you are, Mr Hill," she proffered, "I've given you extra sugar today." It was her way of saying she was sorry for her husband's rudeness and he accepted it as such, even it if did make the tea taste dreadful.

Strangely, the incident did not affect the kindly Mr Hill too adversely. He had been pushed about all of his life; he was used to putting his head down and soldiering on. He gave a small smile to himself as he scraped out the last of the raisins and folded the sack. He may be going home, when at last the shop closed, to a small and meagre home, but his children and grandchildren loved him. Tonight he would sleep with Mrs Hill's arms around him, not only because it helped to keep them both warm in the winter nights, but also because they had always slept like that: like two spoons in a drawer. His face gave an impromptu smile at the thought of the cosiness which lay ahead and he called out quite genuinely to his manager, "Goodnight then Mr Badnell, Mrs Badnell."

On the way home, he caught up with Doreen, "Don't worry about today," he said, "you'll soon get used to him. His bark is worse than his bite."

Doreen thought what a nice man Mr Hill was. She couldn't imagine how he put up with their boss, but she was young and carefree and had never yet had to face an angry rent man or know the humiliation of pawning her wedding ring. She couldn't understand how the elderly assistant could take the rudeness and jibes that he did. But Mr Hill knew what she did not: that he was a genuinely happy man and Tommy Badnell most certainly was not.

Gallery

Tommy Badnell 1916

Walter Gardener
Dearly loved father of Ada and Nellie and
Grandfather of Phil, Kath, Mona and Gladys

Young Ada

Mother and Daughter: Nellie and Kath in Brighton
as taken by Tommy

Tommy as taken by Kathleen in Brighton

Kath, Nellie and Tommy at Woodford Lodge

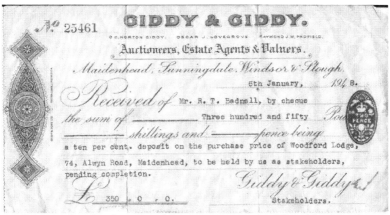

Dances

Dances		Engagements.
1. Waltz		1
2. La Rinka		2
3. Boston Two Step		3
4. Lancers		4
5. Valeta		5
6. Berlin Polka		6
7. Barn Dance		7
8. Waltz Cotillion		8
INTERVAL		INTERVAL
9. Waltz		9
10. Valeta		10
11. Lancers		11
12. Schottische		12
13. La Rinka		13
14. Boston Two Step		14
15. Quadrilles		15
16. Berlin Polka		16
17. Military Two Step		17
18. Waltz and Galop		18

B.T.R's.

Revival Dances

held at the

Ivy Leaf Hall
Marlow Road
Maidenhead

THURSDAYS
8 p.m. till midnight.

M.C's. Mrs. Lamb
Mrs. Roberts
H. G. Burgin
R. T. Badnell

Alec Tyson's Band

BTR Old Time Revival Dance Card

No. 25461

GIDDY & GIDDY.

O.G. HORTON GIDDY.   OSCAR J. LOVEGROVE   RAYMOND J.W. PADFIELD.

Auctioneers, Estate Agents & Valuers.

Maidenhead, Sunningdale, Windsor & Slough.

6th January, 194 8.

Received of Mr. R. T. Badnell, by cheque

the sum of _____ Three hundred and fifty Pou_____

_____ shillings and _____ pence being

a ten per cent. deposit on the purchase price of Woodford Lodge,
74, Alwyn Road, Maidenhead, to be held by us as stakeholders,
pending completion.

£ 350 : 0 : 0.

Giddy & Giddy
Stakeholders.

Receipt for the deposit of the very expensive Woodford Lodge

Nellie, Tommy, Maurice
Ada, Issy, Kath

Chapter 16

Nemesis, I Will Repay

The incident with Mr Hill so soon after the humiliation of the commercial traveller was just too much for Nellie. She had been brought up with genuinely good and Christian parents. Her mother came from Lowestoft where her family had been trawler-men until in one terrible night, in one terrible storm, the men in the family had all perished. Her mother had moved to Merton, near London to work in the lavender fields and had married a young worker in the gun powder mill. He had died when the mill exploded, leaving her pregnant with a child who would die of fits in early manhood.

The family had always been touched by tragedy, hardship and poverty, but in Walter, her new and younger husband, Nellie and Ada's mother had found a gem. Not only was he good-looking and loving, but he also loved their children and was as God-fearing as she and her Norfolk family.

Seeing the deprivation and corruption that drink had brought about in the surrounding areas of London, both were teetotal and when they heard of the movement of Colonel Booth, it seemed made for them.

'My drink is water bright,' the whole family would sing, *'my drink is water bright, from the crystal spring.'*

Unlike other fathers of the day, Walter Gardner never hit his children, well only once: when larking around, one son pushed another's head through the window. Seeing the blood, Walter hit out in anger and desperation but he immediately regretted it. His whole family knew this and never ceased to think of him as anything but the most loving and wonderful father on earth.

When Nellie saw men such as Mr Hill and the Captain humiliated by her husband, she always thought of her dear father; how much he had suffered because he had promised her mother he would never work in the gunpowder mills like his elder brother, her first husband. She could remember his long walks to his badly paid jobs and the winter when they had little to eat but the vegetables he grew in the garden. Somehow it never mattered, for even if there was only bread and dripping, her parents were the type of people who could make a game and pretend that they were eating roast beef, or jelly. If there were only carrots, as there had been one day, then it would be strawberries and cream, only pretend strawberries. But when in the company of her dear dad, nothing ever tasted so wonderful.

The comparison with her husband was almost heart-breaking for Nellie. Dear old Walter had begged her not to marry Tom. Why had she? She knew really. It had been the promise of her own house, her own home. Yet he had cheated her out of that, right at the start of her marriage, he and his witch of a mother. What an evil pair they were, she thought. She had been lured into marriage with a house of which she was never mistress and then used as a slave: force-feeding geese; cleaning; working all hours with no money and no company. She should, of course, have gone back to her dad. He would have taken her back, she knew that. But she would have had to admit that she was wrong, that she had married the wrong man for the wrong reasons.

At least when Ada had come, she had her own family, someone to help. Any passion she had for Tom had gone long ago. It had not lasted for long. After they had returned from their honeymoon and seen his parents sitting in the kitchen window of what had been bought as her home, the reality had struck her within hours. Tom had bought his aged parents a home and she had been brought in as the unpaid servant. Her work as a parlour maid was as nothing to this and no mistress was ever as miserly, spiteful and mean as the wicked old peasant who was her mother-in-law; Nellie felt alone and desperate, bullied and ill-used. Tom never took her part and assumed, along with his mother, that a young wife's lot should be one of toil and obedience. The early years of her marriage, which should have been full of love and anticipation, were some of the worst years of Nellie's life at which time she saw the rest of her life as a prison sentence. Nellie often wondered why the Good Lord had punished her so. The only thing she had ever done wrong in her own eyes was when she was very small and surely that didn't count?

She and her sister Ada had a job, cleaning doorsteps before they went to school each morning, in order to help stretch the family housekeeping. Most of the ladies were very nice and would come out and say, *'That's very nice girls, now off you go to school,'* and would pay them their wages at the end of the week with no trouble. But one woman would always complain and carp. She would point out bits that Nellie had missed, make her whiten the step again and on one dreadful morning, made Nellie late for school. Nellie had never been late for school before and luckily the teacher forgave her. Quite uncharacteristically for Nellie, she felt a great sense of injustice, a sense of anger and need for revenge. So on a day when she knew her tormentor would be away, she went and threw mud all over the doorstep: thick mud she found on the grass verge.

No-one ever found who had spoiled the doorstep and if they did, they did not tell the householder, but the next time Nellie went for her money, there were no complaints and her shilling was given over with no trouble at all.

It was the only thing that Nellie could think of that would make the good Lord punish her. She sometimes thought that God had a very funny way of looking at things. It seemed that sinners managed to get away with an awful lot, whereas she had ended up with a wretched life just because of a muddy doorstep. You only had to read the story of the Prodigal Son to see how unjust the Bible could be. She always felt so sorry for the boy that stayed at home, doing all the work and having none of the fun.

The more Nellie thought about the unfair story of the two brothers, the more other things she had heard at The Army came to mind. Visiting preachers who came to warn them of the evils of drink or allowing their daughters to be drawn into prostitution or worse still the horrors of the White Slave trade frequently wound up their performances (for that is what they were) with the dreaded statement:

'Vengeance is mine, sayeth the Lord. I will repay.'

Now Nellie thought she had waited too long for the Lord to intervene. Another saying was also:

'The Lord helps those who help themselves.'

No-one was a more unlikely Nemesis than Nellie, but she had had enough. Vengeance was going to be hers. She would repay.

The mynah bird had been giving Nellie a lot of irritation.

Even had she not already made up her mind that the loud and evil looking creature was to be the means of her revenge, the squawking of the bird as it constantly showed off its rapidly widening vocabulary was making her nerves worse and worse and the rash on her face was now a constant feature. She always seemed to be scratching and she wondered if the wretched bird might not have mites or ticks or whatever it was feathered creatures had.

Nellie asked her husband if the bird might not have mites and he instantly sorted out a remedy to run through its feathers. He had endless patience with the wretched thing. Far more patience than he ever had with his children, or anyone else come to that.

"You really love that bird don't you Tom?" she probed and his smile towards the bird answered her. Nellie felt that perhaps she should spare the bird, but each time it talked, she could hear the harridan coming through the filthy bead curtains and remembered that dreadful time and the need to balance the books came back to her.

It was one of those strange coincidences that no-one can plan, but on the night that Tom said that the mynah bird was looking a little peaky and he did hope that it was not the effect of the pest powder he had been using, Ada decided that a nice piece of salt beef would make an ideal meal. Ada seemed to like food associated with Jewish cooking and the family never complained as it was always delicious. After the meal, Tom retired to his arm-chair and Nellie helped Ada into the scullery with the dirty dishes. As Ada poured the near boiling water into the sink and added the soda crystals, Nellie carefully removed an off-cut of the salted meat from the side of the dish and wrapping it in her handkerchief; she slipped it into her pocket. Ada caught sight of the hankie and Nellie explained she thought she was about to sneeze, "You know what I'm like if there is any pepper about."

Later that evening she went up the stairs, found her eyebrow tweezers in her dressing table drawer and crept down the two flights of stairs to the shop.

Very carefully Nellie lifted a corner of the cage cover. She took out the piece of meat and using the tweezers, put the meat into the cage before dropping the cover again and climbing the stairs to re-join the rest of the family.

The bird was feeling ill. She had nearly choked when all that dust had been put through her feathers. Her senses were not as sharp as usual. She could smell something. Perhaps her Tommy had come to put some cheese in to tempt her. She fluttered down to the bottom of the cage and picked it up. It wasn't cheese; it was delicious and she tore at it.

A short while later, the bird knew that she was dying; it was not Tommy's dust that was killing her, it was the titbit at the bottom of the cage and the bird knew who had left it: the small, smiling creature who was her enemy.

Tommy was devastated the next morning when he found the body of the bird on the bottom of the cage. He blamed himself for using the mite powder. He blamed Nellie for going on and on about mites and pests.

"It's your fault, you stupid woman," he shouted harshly and just as she was about to think that her secret was discovered, he added, "If you hadn't been so particular, the bird would be alright; just as she was really starting to talk, just as she was sitting on my hand." A large tear rolled down his face as he cradled the dead bird in his hands. Nellie had never seen her husband display so much compassion. It was typical of him to weep over a bird but think nothing of the hurt he had caused her. She said nothing. There was really nothing to say. They would never be even. She could never be fully revenged on a man who had caused her so much humiliation and misery; so much that even one of the sweetest of natures had been driven to kill a harmless bird out of frustration and hurt.

Ada heard Tom's cry of anguish and sensing a catastrophe had descended to the shop. Seeing Tom's misery she instinctively put her arm around him and said quite genuinely, "I'm so sorry, Tom, I know how much that bird meant to you."

"Well at least there will be no more mites or bugs now," came the reply, "So someone will be pleased." And turning to his wife, he called out, "Well, you'll be pleased then Nellie, the poor thing always knew you hated her, but she knew I loved her, poor little thing." The tears continued to roll down his face and he cradled the bird like a child; strange, since he had had little time for either of his children as infants.

Chapter 17

The White Cottage

Oh yes, Nellie should have gone home to her dad after the first betrayal. Now she was in her forties, she would go whilst she still could. Everything was welling up inside her. The old witch's face, the captain's cough as he trudged up the High Street with her half-crown in his pocket, and dear Mr Hill who had helped her so much when Tom was away and who put up with everything so well. She almost felt as if she was going to faint or vomit. Every time she closed her eyes she saw the dead bird in her husband's hands and his look of accusation. The itch on her face was constant. It seemed to spread over the whole of her body. She knew that if she had to share that double bed again with him she would scream or throw herself in the river, plenty of women did. She couldn't bear the thought of having to look at him or touch him ever again. Without telling anyone and not really knowing what she was doing, she put down the bread knife, took her coat from behind the door and walked down the stairs, through the shop and out through the door.

"Where are you going Nellie?" called Tommy as he laid another wafer thin rasher on the pile. "What about the tea?"

But Nellie didn't care about the tea. She was doing what she should have done over twenty years ago: going back to her dad who loved her, who never betrayed her and who, like Mr Hill, was *'one of nature's gentlemen.'*

It was not far to the White Cottage where old Walter had come to be near his two beautiful daughters and live with his granddaughter Mona. He had bought two oval pictures which reminded him of them or of how they could have been. The two young women, so like Helen and Ada, leant from open windows awaiting messages of love brought by doves. How cruel life was, he thought. He had hoped to protect them both and now they both lived with a man he could neither admire nor trust, a man who had cheated them both and there was little an old man like him could do. At least in the White cottage they had somewhere to come and see their old dad. He loved to hear them sing, *'We shall gather at the river'* or *'my drink is water bright,'* just as they had when girls. He supposed they had both wanted security, money, homes. Now Nellie owned a home but the situation of both his girls was untenable. Tom may have plenty of money and several houses but his two girls could be out at any time and then what would become of them?

Mr Lloyd George had given them all the old age pension, but he couldn't support them all on that. Old Walter was almost as respected in his own way as the late Miss Poupard and he knew that he had to do something for his daughters. He wasn't quite certain what, but the later events of the evening when Nellie put down the bread knife and walked out of the door helped him to make up his mind. Tommy Badnell may well be a crafty little peasant but the good Lord would guide Walter. He was his strength and his redeemer and he knew that with divine help he could get justice for his girls from his son-in-law. He must try to do what was right and resolve the situation as best he could.

Walter heard his daughter's footsteps on the path. He knew at once that it was Nellie, but something was wrong. She was staggering and anyway it was not her night to come. He had washed and dried her hair only last week. It wouldn't be washed again for another month; just rubbed with a silk handkerchief to take the grease away and make it shine. She had the loveliest hair – thick and glossy like a bird's wing.

He rose from his chair as quickly as he could. He was an old man now and as he opened the door, she collapsed into his arms. The bond between them was so great that he knew, she had no need to tell him, she was breaking down under the strain. The early years of abuse and ill-treatment by Tom's mother and the latter years of running the shop, living in cramped and stifling circumstances had finally taken their toll. Tom did not keep either of them short, but their lives were oppressed and stilted now. They had both enjoyed themselves so much whilst he was away.

Walter laid his younger daughter on the couch and covered her with the rug which had been over his knees until he heard her. He went next door and asked the young lad to run and fetch the doctor as quickly as possible and by eleven that night, Nellie was in the

Cottage Hospital. She had succumbed to a complete breakdown and would not be discharged for at least three months. Tom could no longer ignore his wife's unhappiness and desperation although he was puzzled as to why she had, in his eyes, suddenly and completely collapsed.

Ada carried on in her doggedly determined way looking after them all and wondered how the whole tragic business might have been avoided. Kath and Phil carried on with the lives as before; Auntie was still there to provide for them and their emotional lives had taken off, away from the family and the three fraught adults with whom they lived. Kath was aware that her young man's parents were still wrapped up in one another. In fact, to Maurice's embarrassment, his mother was expecting her sixth child; she was after all married to a man seven years her junior and they had a great passion for one another. Kath could see the difference. The way the lady's eyes sparkled in a way her own mother's never did. As for Phil, his future family were a jolly lot held together with strong but kindly bonds by the redoubtable Mrs P, capable, long-suffering and endlessly resilient.

Old Walter grieved. He grieved that his daughter should have suffered so; that she had not come to him before. He grieved that she had married Tom, been cheated by his whole ghastly family, but most of all he grieved for her beautiful hair. For the morning after she had been admitted to the cottage hospital the night nurse had found her hair on the pillow. The shining bird's wing, her crowning glory, lay at the bottom of a cardboard box which the sister handed to him. She had coiled it up, as it had once lain on the top of her patient's head and she handed it with a sad smile to the person she instinctively knew loved Nellie best of all.

Nellie herself felt a great sense of relief to be away from the shop. She had a little side room and the doctor ordered that she must be kept very quiet. Only her father was to visit initially. Tactfully, the husband and children were told that no visitors at all were allowed. So Walter and Nellie had hours of tranquillity, sitting together saying nothing, simply remembering in unspoken union the joy of those hard early days in Merton, hiding beneath the table to eat their bread and dripping, pretending it was roast beef and Yorkshire puddings.

Walter had never had the resources that his son-in-law enjoyed and he did not own his own home until he was in his old age, but he had loved and cared for his wife. She had her funny little ways he recalled, but she made him so happy. They had led good lives going to the Army, watching in admiration as Nellie had waved her tambourine and sung, *'My drink is water bright, from the crystal spring.'* Nellie looked at her dad from under the frill of the little cap which Auntie Blossie had stitched for her. The old milliner had shown her love and sympathy in every little stitch. She had made it from the finest of lawn, for as she explained to Walter, she did not want it to rub and she had embroidered lily of the valley on it; so very, very kind.

Nellie became a firm favourite in the hospital. She liked to help with the mending of the hospital gowns and towels and the sisters were glad of her dainty stitches and her quiet sweet nature. Nellie thought that it must be rather like being a nun; everything clean and quiet, no noisy men and no having to share a bed with one snoring and belching and smelling of Guinness or rum and milk. In all honesty Tom was not a drunk but to Ada and Nellie, brought up in the midst of the temperance movement, anything but a small sherry at Christmas time seemed excessive. They both wished fervently that the shop did not have an off licence, although both agreed that it was the off licence that made the profit and which brought in the high class customers. Even Ivor Novello had once rung the bell in the middle of the night and asked Tom in the nicest and most dramatic way for a bottle of whisky, whilst also reminding him not to allow his mother too much; and who in their right mind would refuse a gentleman who could write songs like his?

Chapter 18

The Jewel

Nellie had moved into her Dad's house. Her long stay in hospital followed by a long recuperation at the White Cottage nursed by her father and her sweet natured niece Mona, had restored her health and her calm. Ada and Tom visited her daily and seeing her composed and happy, Tom realised just how lovely she still was and how much he missed her. When she was there all the time he took her for granted, never fully comprehending how much she contributed to their home life and the successful running of the business. Now that she had been away for so long he realised just how much he would miss her if she left for good. Seeing how content she, her father and her niece were, he wondered if she would ever return and a sense of real panic came to him now that he was forced to face up to the possibility of losing her.

It was whilst she felt safe; whilst she sensed that for once she had the upper hand that Nellie decided to tell him about her home ownership. It was only because Tom always left the running of the business to herself and Ada that she had been able to keep her secret from him for so long. Now she felt it was a good time to tell Tommy who was, after all, her husband; a woman should not have secrets from her partner. She also wanted him to know that she, unlike many other married women, was not entirely vulnerable. She was a woman of property and he must treat her with respect. Tom's reaction to the news was unexpected. As she told him about the bonus of how with old Mr Kilby's help she had invested it, Tom's face took on a look of incredulity and then of deep hurt and sorrow.

"Why didn't you tell me Nellie?" he asked.

"Because you would have been angry and shouted - said I'd cheated you."

"Why couldn't you trust me?"

Her face changed. The eczema flared up over her eyebrow. The tranquillity that had surrounded her when he came in disappeared,

"Trust, trust," she said in a despairing and anguished way, "I trusted you with our first house, it was never mine. You let your mother treat me like a slave; she even begrudged me the eggs from our own hens. I worked day and night. She wouldn't even get me a doctor when I was having young Phil, just because she could deliver her own babies. I can never trust you Tom. You have betrayed me in every way a man could. I really don't know if I can ever bear to go back to the shop again. If you really want the truth, I can't stand you. I only said I'd marry you because I thought you'd go to Canada."

She started to twist her handkerchief between her hands. She avoided him with her eyes and added, "I think it best if I stay here with Dad. I'm happy here Tom and it's been a very long time since I've been happy."

Tom could feel the tears welling up. He had never realised just how miserable she was. She was right, he had betrayed her in so many ways and now, just when after all these years she had decided to leave him, he realised what he had neglected for so long: his wife, the mother of his children; his partner and one of the prettiest and smartest women in the town.

Tom got up and went out through the kitchen, avoiding old Walter and as soon as he was in the dark lane outside, he let the tears flow. He leant against the railings and sobbed as he had never sobbed before. Nellie was good and beautiful and kind and everyone with half a grain of sense knew it. But he had treated her so badly. He had made her ill and sad and now he had lost her. He blew his nose and wiped his eyes. He must do something. He would get her back. He would change. He would show his appreciation and affection for her. He would stop paying attention to Ada and young Doreen. He would show Nellie that she was as lovely as the days when she worked in the laundry. He tried to think of what had pleased her in those early days and remembered the opal ring. She had really liked that ring until his mother had told her it was unlucky.

Being the youngest, Tommy's mother had always had more time for him than her other children. She had what sometimes almost passed as affection for him. With all her other children, there had always been another on the way very quickly and in the early days her life had been one of almost desperate drudgery. She had married very young; she herself was not quite certain what age she was and

97

she was immediately pregnant. She had to work to earn money by milking the cows belonging to the farmer whose cottage they rented and she had to draw the water from the well, until she had children old and strong enough to do it for her.

The nearest place to shop for things which she could not produce herself was Maidenhead and that was a good six mile walk. Often she could get a ride on the back of a cart but more often than not she had to walk a good part of the journey alone hauling her purchases with her. By the time she had Tommy things were easier. She had more time for him and she loved to hear him recite poems. Not that she ever let him know, for poems and reading kept him from collecting the eggs or helping with the harvest and supporting the family budget.

Although he may have been her favourite, Tommy now realised what he had missed; he had never had the closeness, the concern that old Walter showed for Nellie and Ada. His mother had never caressed him, never mind kissed him. He remembered the time when he had come home screaming and crying because he had lost the end of his little finger when he fell through the hayloft floor. Clouting him across the head, she had sent him back to the hayloft to find the fingertip. True, when he got back she had collected several clean cobwebs from the hedgerow and had managed to secure the tip of his finger on again where it still grew like a little ram's horn; but there had been no comforting, no soothing words. He knew that Nellie called his mother the old witch and he wondered if she knew just how near to the truth that was. He remembered people coming to the cottage to have their warts charmed; he thought maybe they had come for other reasons too.

Tommy really had grown up in the hard school of knocks he decided. He remembered his oldest brother coming home from the Boer War. He could remember the excitement when the headmaster had come into the classroom and announced that Badnell was to go straight home as his brother had come home from the war. Tommy had run all the way home expecting to find a hero, but slumped in the chair was the wreck of the young plough boy who had left.

Tom's fine soldier brother was in the last stages of dysentery and even his mother's healing powers could not save him. She had already felt his head and his stomach and knew that this son she could never save. She felt a strange feeling inside for he was her firstborn and they had been young together. When Tommy had asked his mother in the barn how long his brother would take to get better, she had replied, "The officers have sent him home to die; that's what they've done, sent him home to die. No more use for him see; can't have soldiers with dysentery, no damn use to anyone."

It was as if his mother agreed with the officers. It was just like when he came in and said that the hens were not laying; he knew his mother would be wringing their necks in the next few days. Once something was useless it had to go. Tommy looked at his mother's hard fixed face and decided to leave the barn before he let the tears roll down his cheeks.

"Tommy," his brother had said when asked if the Boers were very fierce, "they were just like us. They were ploughboys and farmers. They weren't any different at all; and Ma, what we did to those women and children..." He shook his head and slumped further into the chair.

He didn't talk much; he was too weak, but once he brightened a little and giving Tommy a wink, he said somewhat prophetically, "When you're in battle Tommy, never mind the enemy, it's the officers you want to look out for."

He died soon after that and Tommy's mum took it as she took everything. She didn't weep. She seemed not to mourn; keeping all her feelings, if indeed she had any, to herself. To the outside world, she presented herself as a harsh, mean and at times quite violent old peasant, hitting children, dogs and horses who annoyed her as the mood took her. For an up and coming man like Tommy, she was becoming – had become – a total embarrassment.

There were times when he detested his mother. She didn't fit in anymore; dreadful old woman hitting people with her stick and still insisting on wearing her bustle. He hadn't realised that Nellie had wanted a doctor and it was his mother who had denied her one. That made him angry. He could have lost his son and his wife. He would put his mother into rooms somewhere and he would buy Nellie something nice.

He was about to cross the road to the shop, when he noticed the illuminated windows in Biggs. A pretty ring of sapphires caught his eye. Beneath it a discreet message read, *'sapphires for everlasting love.'* The price beneath was of course quite exorbitant but he always said, *'you've got to speculate to accumulate.'* If he wanted Nellie back, speculate he must and he would. He felt brighter now that he had a project. He would buy the ring for Nellie and perhaps he would look for a property where they could live together as a family. That should do the trick. As he pulled the door key from his pocket, he saw the constable trying the doors further up the road and called out cheerily, "I've just been looking out a welcome home present for the missus."

He knew now what he must do; he must woo her again, win her back. The family, the customers and he needed her. After all, what a fool he would look if his wife went off to live in her own smart house in Fielding Road. Now that would give people something to talk about. He put the key in the door and started to give a cheery whistle. Things were going to be fine; or as they had started to say, *'just fine and dandy.'*

Inevitably, Tommy got his way in the end but he had to work quite hard to persuade Nellie to return to the shop. Strangely, his greatest ally turned out to be his father-in-law. Although Walter had done his utmost to convince Nellie at the time of her marriage to Tommy that it was a big mistake, he had said to her, "Marriage is forever. If you take this step you must live with it," and he had left the prayer book open at the page of the marriage service to emphasise the point. Neither he nor his wife had attended the wedding and it had been left to Nellie's aunt to provide the wedding gown and what little family support there had been. It was strange, but his wife's parents had not attended her first marriage and although she remembered so well the pain that had caused, neither parent felt able to condone what they knew to be a disastrous union with their presence. Now that Tommy was constantly asking her to return, Walter said one evening that it was time she went. He reassured her of his love for her; told her that she could come as often as she wanted, but that she must return to her family.

Nellie was a little shocked and very saddened that her dear Dad who she loved so much was sending her home and seeing her crestfallen face he whispered,

"Those whom God had joined together..." He was right of course; he always was and she should have listened to him but it did seem unfair that one had to spend the rest of one's life paying for a youthful mistake.

Walter of course was not going to allow Nellie back into a situation that would ruin her health again and he decided that for once he would interfere just a little. Things were not right. Both of his daughters had been brought up in the army; they had been told that only the highest of moral standards ever brings about happiness and yet here they were in the most dreadful muddle. Thank Goodness his dear wife had been promoted to Glory.

The next time that Tommy came round to see Nellie; Walter met him down the lane. He knew that he must handle things carefully; he had the feeling that his son-in-law wanted things to be better and more than anything, before he too was promoted to higher things, he wanted to make sure that his little girls were going to be happy. It was not only them he had to think of now, there were also his granddaughters to think of: Mona and Kath. He felt so frustrated; there was no reason why all of their lives could not be fulfilled and happy. If only things had been slightly different. If Ada had married Tom she could have handled him and his family and Nellie would have happily helped them and worked in the shop. Everyone said she was an excellent business woman, but she was not cut out to be Tom's wife. Nevertheless, that was what she was and they must all try to make the best of things.

Tom saw his father-in-law coming and wondered why, on this occasion, he had decided to meet him. He felt some apprehension but the old man gave him a friendly smile and said encouragingly, "Well Tom, you won't be doing this walk for much longer. Nellie will soon be well enough to come home." He paused and they strolled on a little way.

"Of course Nellie will have to take things easy for a long while. She can't have anything emotional or upsetting and she will need to be cossetted and nursed."

After another short pause he added, "Or she will have to come back and stay here with me, or of course I suppose, she could always go and live in Fielding Road. It's very peaceful up there and Ada

101

could always go and care for her. They have always been very close my girls."

He turned so that he blocked the younger man's path and added in a more forthright tone, "You do know what I mean, don't you?"

Tommy did and he was glad that he had made his purchase that day, it would show the old man that he meant to change. He was glad that he had gone to the bank on the corner and withdrawn the nice large white five pound notes and gone into Biggs and bought his token of everlasting love. He was even more pleased that it was in his pocket in its beautiful black box, lined in white silk, with the words Biggs of Maidenhead discreetly printed on the inside lid. He had been amazed at the blueness of the stones, the colour of cornflowers or the sky on a summer's day. It was very different from when he had bought the opals from the Old Jew in Market Street.

"An excellent colour," the salesman had said, "and a plain but very fashionable setting. Any lady of any age would be delighted with such a jewel."

Tommy had got quite a thrill being spoken to in this way. It was true money may not be everything, but it certainly bought you respect.

"It's for my wife," he started, "she's been ill and I wanted to let her know ..."

His eyes filled with tears. It so annoyed him when this happened, but the salesman was quite touched, and with the tact which his job demanded he said, indicating a small gold chair, "If you would care to sit down, I will find you a nice little box and have your jewel wrapped."

Tommy liked the word jewel; he liked it even more that he was buying one. Who would have thought that little Tommy from Knowl Hill was buying a jewel? It lay safely in his pocket and he brought it out and showed it to his father-in-law, "It's a jewel," he said, "it's for Nellie. They are sapphires and they are a sign of everlasting love."

Old Walter thought that there were many signs of everlasting love and thank goodness they didn't all have to come from Biggs. If that had been the case, he would never have been able to show his love for his own dear wife. But he smiled at Tommy, knowing he meant well and said,

"It's beautiful Tommy. I'm sure Nellie will love it but you must show her you love her in your actions. Nellie has always been the sensitive one, she's very ... fragile I suppose, not like Ada. Nellie should really have been an artist. She could always draw you know. Not just the little doodles she does now. Nellie could really draw."

He shook his head. Perhaps unwittingly he had contributed to his daughter's unhappiness. Surprisingly, he found himself confiding in his son-in-law. He told him of how he remembered the time when Nellie had been in service, working as a parlour maid, "She was so pretty."

After the way that Ada had disappeared from their lives, Walter had made sure that Nellie was placed with a good and Christian family. The head of the house was a professor and his wife worked for the rights of the poor and for women's education. He had managed to speak to them both and emphasised that his wife came from a well-to-do family in Norfolk. He had no intention of another daughter being taken advantage of. He was aware of the white slave trade; they often talked about it in the Army. Salvation Army officers were always on the lookout for young girls in distress.

Tommy nodded in agreement. He had also been concerned about Kathleen. He had wanted her to stay in the shop and work, where he could keep an eye on her, but she had insisted on working in London. Walter continued his story of paternal concern and regret and of how his amazement and horror knew no bounds when, after a year or so in service, on her day off, Nellie arrived home accompanied by a much older man; a gentleman it is true, who said he was a friend of her employers. He said that he had seen her draw and wanted to take her to his college to study art. Art? Whoever heard of a parlour maid studying art?

Walter had known exactly what his game was.

All the time that he was speaking, Tommy nodded his agreement. Daughters were difficult. It seemed that whatever you did was wrong. He certainly had no sway in what young Kathleen did, but he had put his foot down about paying for her to go to art school. Who did the little madam think she was? Old Walter well-remembered the conversation he had with Nellie's companion.

"I assure you sir, your daughter has a natural and pronounced talent," the gentleman had said.

"And how might you know?" Walter had retorted.

"I know," continued the gentleman, "because I am the head of the drawing school at the Slade School of Art and I am offering your daughter a great opportunity."

Walter had looked at the man. He looked aloof, a little strange, but basically a good man, a gentleman. But then all of the warnings he had heard came flooding back to him: the warnings of young girls being taken off to be governesses and companions and never being seen again. Walter could not risk it, not with his Nellie. How could he let her go and live in Chelsea? He could not risk his beautiful daughter's safety so he said, "The likes of you must think we come up from piss. Well we don't! And you can tell your fine friends that they can look for a new parlour maid. Nellie is never going back there if you are the sort of company they keep."

He really could not believe that he had spoken like that; in that common way. It reminded him of the time when his sons had larked about and one of his sons' heads had gone through the window. It was the only time he had ever hit them; but he had been so worried. And he had been worried about Nellie, in a different way, but just as much.

Looking back, Walter could see that with the best will in the world, he may have barred his daughter from a path which could have led to great happiness and fulfilment, for he had found out soon afterwards that the Slade was indeed a famous Art School. He had also discovered that the school's new principal was a friend of his daughter's former employers. Of course had she gone to the Slade, she would never have gone to the laundry.

Revealing all of this to Tom seemed strange, but in many ways they were now in the same position. Both had caused Nellie unhappiness. Both wanted to make amends, and both had the natural concerns of fathers. In a short walk they had formed a fragile and unexpected alliance.

"I don't think either of us has made poor Nellie happy, we must try, we really must. Next time, I really think she could throw herself in the river."

So, they arrived at the cottage together and to Nellie's amazement and Walter's surprised delight, Tommy knelt beside Nellie's chair and putting his arm around her waist he kissed her very gently and with great tenderness on the cheek.

"I have something for you Nellie, to show you that I do love you and I will try to make you happy." He gave her the black leather box and when she opened it a look of spontaneous pleasure lit up her face.

"Oh Tom," she beamed, "it's so beautiful."

She turned and kissed him, feeling real pleasure.

"Then you'll come back?" he asked tentatively. She glanced down again at the blueness of the sapphires and answered, "Yes. It's time I got back. I'll come back Sunday afternoon … in time for tea."

Chapter 19

Biggs

Bill and Olive Pragnell who kept the greengrocers just up the High Street from Kilby's, had a very jolly family. Mrs P. as she was always known, was a wonderful cook and manager, skills she passed on to her daughters Olive and Margery. Olive soon became attached to and later married Phil and their son George became an apprentice at Biggs. He had a great affinity for gems and beautiful things and later founded a famous jewellery shop in Stratford on Avon.

Biggs was directly opposite Kilby's which benefitted both shops and often people visiting the grocer's would unexpectedly see celebrities or even royalty visiting the jewellers. The only problem lay with the fact that women of taste like Nellie soon discovered the difference between real jewels and run of the mill bijouterie.

Nellie looked down at her hand. Of course she could not appear in the shop without a wedding band. That would be improper and cause gossip. On her return from Brighton, she had sent Ada out to buy a cheap ring from the local pawn shop but now she stood looking in the window of Biggs.

'New, beautiful twenty-two carat bevelled wedding bands' read the small discreet sign. And they were beautiful. Compared to what she had on her hand. No ugly edges, not too yellow, not too pink. Modern … what was the word? … Chic. She looked at the price tag and decided it didn't matter. She turned back, changed her dress and powdered her nose and taking the five pound notes from under the mattress, she walked down the stairs, past the door to the living room, through the shop, across the road and into the other world that was Biggs. She sat on a small gold chair basking in the soothing luxury and waited for the smart young salesman to say,

"And how may I help you Madam?"

"I lost my wedding ring on holiday in Brighton," smiled Nellie, "I should like to replace it without my husband knowing." She and the young salesman exchanged a conspiratorial smile, "The new ones, the twenty-two carat gold ones," she said.

After a pleasant time spent trying on, discussing the colour of the gold and the smoothness of the design, Nellie left the shop wearing a ring she had chosen and paid for herself. It was beautiful and it didn't leave her finger until it was cut off in her very old age. It was her bond with herself and the best that money could buy. It didn't worry her that no-one noticed, in fact she was pleased. Another little secret to keep to herself, but the date stamped inside registered the lowest point of her life: 1927, said the stamp, 22 carat. Whenever she felt down she thought of that; she couldn't quite work out why, but it meant something. She gave a little smile to herself. Life had a funny way of turning out.

Chapter 20

Charlie and Nellie

Neither Ada nor Nellie realised that Tommy stayed in the cellar because he had come to realise that his company was not welcome upstairs. He went up for his meals; went up in time to go to bed, but he rarely sat with the family for long. He was comfortable in the cellar; he had a chair now, a glass, an electric light and of course his westerns. Westerns were Tom's fantasy world - the Wild West: stagecoaches, cowboys, horses and saloons. If Tom had a good Western, he could escape. Of course he should be living the life. Every time he received a letter from his friend Charlie, he knew he should have gone. He shouldn't have been such a coward. He had met Charlie when he joined Kilby's. Charlie wasn't gentry at all but his parents were different from the two old peasants who had brought Tommy into the world. Charlie's parents didn't just want him to make money, they wanted him to have a better life and by the sound of his letters, a better life was what Charlie had.

Charlie was a great reader of newspapers. He knew what was going on. Charlie was aware of gold rushes but was far too sensible to buy a pick and pan and follow the crowd. Charlie heard about prospectors and loggers and trappers and he remembered what they had both been taught as grocery apprentices - everyone needs groceries: in peace, in war, in good times and hard time, people need groceries.

"Tom," he had said one day, "Canada is opening up. It is the perfect place for us. All these farmers and loggers, they will all need food, fodder for their beasts, work clothes, pans and tools. Tom, you and I would make a great team. No-one knows groceries like me and you are so good with the animals; you know all the remedies, all about harness and tack. Tom, together we will make a fortune; be a great success. Europe does nothing but fight. You and I will always be looked down on by the gentry with plums in their mouths, but in

Canada, we can be somebody. It's a new country, let's go before we get bogged down, before it's too late."

Tom sensed his friend's enthusiasm. He knew that Charlie was right because Charlie always was. Charlie had introduced Tom to baths: cold baths. He told him tactfully about his dress, the need for clean underwear. In fact had Charlie not been part of Tom's life, neither would Nellie.

Nellie did not want to marry Tom. Nellie knew what it was to be in love and she knew that she did not love Tom. Nellie has been in love, in fact still was in love, with a boy she had met at the seaside. He was just the sort of boy she knew her parents would approve of. He was studying to be a cabinet maker and like her own family, he came from a non-conformist family. They believed in education, questioning the power of the gentry. They believed that drink and ignorance kept the poor in poverty and that this was what the ruling classes wanted. Both Nellies' parents believed in temperance and education, they also believed in fun and a better life for all.

The young man that Nellie had met for a long weekend at Clacton-on-Sea made it all seem so simple, so right. He came from a simple family but his parents knew that things were going to change, that their children would have a better life and they wanted that better life soon. The young man recognised in Nellie a natural gentility, a grace and charm, a lightness of speech and a complete trust in himself that he knew he wanted to be in his life forever.

Nellie and the young man began a correspondence which grew over several months into an understanding which both knew would end in a proposal and acceptance of marriage as soon as he became a master cabinet maker. He had already decided on the piece of furniture that he would make for her as an engagement present.

Then the letters stopped; quite suddenly. There was no cooling, no quarrel. Nellie knew that he had loved her. They had only spent such a short time together after their eyes had met across the crowd at the band stand, but they had both known, definitely, for sure, there would never be anyone else, ever. They were the same sort of people, they just knew; and so the letters had been enough and through them they planned their future: the cottage; the workshop; the good and loving life which they would share together. Then nothing; no letter, her letters were not returned. She was left with only sorrow, loss and numbing heartbreak.

Soon afterwards, Tommy had come into the laundry shop. The first time he came in, he was dressed in his country clothes: very neat and very clean, but they marked him out as a country boy. On his head he had a beige felt cap. It was smart and new but most of the young men in the town wore boaters in the summer and felt hats such as those favoured by the king, in the winter. Round his neck he wore a large cravat, also in beige. It was tied in quite an ornate way and the watch chain he wore across his waistcoat, quite high up, was gold; quite unusual for a country lad so young. He wore boots that were also of good quality such as a farmer might wear and outside he left his real treasure, the envy of many of the male passers-by, his prize whippet with which he coursed at the weekends. It was a large, broad-chested beast and a champion. Tommy was dressed the way that he was and had the whippet with him because they had been to the photographers. The dog was a champion and it was because of his winning ways that Tommy sported a gold Albert. The dog lived all week with Tom's parents. He knew that as long as the dog won and could catch the odd hare and rabbit for his mother's pot, he would be well cared for. His mother did not believe in maintaining useless animals – or humans come to that – although she had healing skills and many people visited her to have their warts charmed.

For once, his cheeky country ways deserted him and he was awed by the looks and speech of the new young lady at the counter. She didn't look like a working girl. She was so lovely, so refined. He rushed back to Charlie who left their digs immediately to confirm his friend's impressions of the new girl. Charlie agreed that the new laundry assistant was the loveliest creature that he or Tommy were ever likely to come across.

For a while, Tommy was concerned that his friend's sophistication might steal a march on him, but this was not the case. Charlie's sights were set on Canada. He would find a wife eventually, but not in Maidenhead and not in 1906; that would all come later when he was rich and in another country.

The problem for Charlie was that he did want Tommy to come with him. He knew Tommy's skill with horses and mules and he knew that if his dream to set up a chain of dry goods stores was to flourish, he needed those skills. They would not just come in handy, they would be a necessity!

The younger man's infatuation was understandable but he hoped it would pass. He hoped this not only for himself, but also for his friend. Tommy was the youngest child of a pair of ghastly, greedy, small-minded peasants; it was fairly obvious in fact that his mother was a gypsy. If Tommy wanted to make his way in the world, learn to dress correctly, speak well and make his fortune, the more distance he could put between himself and his dreadful mother the better. Charlie just wished that the beautiful girl at the laundry had delayed taking up her post until after he and his partner were aboard ship and sailing for the colonies.

Tommy had other ideas, in fact only one idea. He wanted Nellie. Like many men who are the baby of the family, what Tommy wanted, Tommy had to have. He had to have Nellie.

At this point, high fashion decided to play an important role in their lives. Nellie, despite having limited money, was always dressed in the height of fashion and Tommy was always up to the minute with music hall songs. He bought the song sheets and was always word perfect within a few days.

Nellie, always hopeful that a letter would arrive inviting her to Clacton-on-Sea, had bought a hat; a special hat which had almost put her into debt. It was straw and curving from front to back were two great white wings – as if a sea bird were nesting within the straw crown. The whiteness of the straw and the feathers showed off the brown smoothness of her hair as it swept up from her neck above her high starched collar.

Tommy had taken to waiting outside the laundry and following Nellie home, he had tried to talk to her but she would have nothing to do with him. Now the effect of walking behind her: her hair; the feather wings and the narrowness of her waist, made him more than ever determined to make her his girl; in fact to marry her. He had to have her: her softness, smallness, he had to possess the thing about her that would always escape him. It was what the gentry had and no-one in his family ever would.

It happened that just at that time, the favourite song in the music halls was *'White Wings'*. Tommy would follow Nellie at first

111

humming the tune but when she made no response, not even turning around, he started to sing the words,

'White Wings they never grow weary,
They carry me cheerily over the sea,
White wings they never grow weary,
Oh carry my loved one home safely to me.'

Tommy did not know it but at first all that Nellie could think of was the seaside and the lovely young man who had suddenly stopped writing to her. Whenever she thought about him, a strange longing came over her and she ended up by hugging her pillow and weeping into it. She wished this wretched young man would stop following her and singing to her; she felt so foolish. What must people think?

What people thought was soon made clear to Nellie. Many of the ladies who called into the laundry told her how they had noticed what a devoted admirer she had: how smart he was, such a nice young man. He had a good job at Kilby's and one said that he was about to emigrate to Canada with his friend and she would miss out on a good catch if she didn't' stop being so snooty.

Nellie thought about it. She was over twenty and not yet married. She had had an understanding, but this had come to nothing. The woman was right. She must look to her future and perhaps it wouldn't hurt to go out with the young man who sang to her. Some people thought it was romantic.

Nellie just wanted a letter with a Clacton-on-Sea postmark. She made up her mind that if a letter did not arrive in the next week, she would give up and start at the very least to smile at the young man who waited outside the laundry each evening. Perhaps he was very nice when you got to know him. There would never be what she had had with John, that glance across the bandstand and knowing for sure, forever, that this was the one. She just could not understand what had happened. She had written again and again asking what she had done, why he had forgotten her. She had realised that maybe he had had to change his digs and had written all over her letters.

"Please, please forward." But still no letter had come.

Nellie told her aunt of her dilemma. Should she hang on to the chance, now fading, of true love or start to walk out with other suitors?

Nellie's aunt, like most women of that time, was a pragmatist. She knew how pathetic women who remained unmarried were, without homes of their own and no children. It was fine if one was lucky enough to be placed like Miss Poupard, who lived on Kidwell's Park. The only child of wealthy parents, she would always be provided for. She had a maid to do the work whilst she painted her water colours and visited the sick. She was a nice woman but she did not have to face the realities of life as Nellie had to. A young man who had prospects and ambition was a good catch, even if it did look as if he had some gypsy blood in him. He clearly adored Nellie and perhaps if only she would walk out with him, she would forget this John at the seaside and start thinking about houses and babies. That, after all, was what marriage was really about.

So Nellie very tentatively started to talk to Tom and in time agreed to let him walk with her. His persistence meant that things moved on swiftly: walking to the bandstand by the river, having tea by the river, even going on a punt on the river. Maidenhead has always been a good place for courting in the summer months.

Tommy wanted to get to the point of asking Nellie to marry him quickly. The reason was not entirely ardour. He wanted to ask her to marry him and go to Canada before Charlie left.

Charlie had been pressing on with his plans to emigrate for some time now. He had books about Canada, maps and timetables. He bought magazines showing the wildlife of the country: the huge bears and moose, the wolves and eagles. Tom was entranced. He knew all of the animals that lived in Berkshire. He knew where they could be found and how they could be snared or caught. He knew the cry of the birds and which ones went in winter and returned as if by magic each spring. Tommy looked at the pictures of covered wagons pulled by teams of horses. He was fascinated at which breeds they used. He knew that his skills with mules would be put to good use in a place like that. His old dad was a carter and what he and his sons did not know about draught beast was scarcely worth knowing.

Charlie bought his flannel shirts. They were checked and colourful, quite unlike anything he would have worn in England. He also packed several long white aprons to wear in the store which he was going to open. He wanted, he said, to bring the gentility of Maidenhead High Street to the Wild West. No-one had any doubt that he would succeed. Certainly, Tommy had no doubts. Charlie was one of those men who thought big. He did not just want to make money, he wanted to make things better. Charlie wanted a new, clean, good life. He did not want the gentry telling him what to do, He had little time for the upper classes.

"A lot of inbred idiots," was how he had described them to a shocked Tommy who had been brought up to touch his cap to almost everyone. Years later, Tom was to remember those words in Italy and wish that he had followed his friend's advice.

"Leave Europe," he said. "It's finished - nothing but wars, in which we shall have to fight. The upper classes still treat us like cattle and no space, Tom. No space to breathe and walk. Look at us all crammed into tiny houses. Look at the two of us, sharing a room and look at those poor devils in the Barracks. People should not have to live like that. Did you know that the Romans had baths thousands of years ago?"

Charlie knew so much. He knew about Canada and the Romans. Tom knew the poem about some Romans who had defended a bridge but he did not know that they had baths.

He could have listened to Charlie all night and Charlie would have talked to him and told him things he had read or what his mother, who had been a governess, had told him. But their landlady liked to get her sleep. The walls of the digs were thin and she told them in no uncertain terms to be quiet. Both of the young men pressed on with their plans. Charlie ordered his trunk and began to fill it. He told Mr Kilby his plans and thanked him for the excellent training which he had received at the shop. He did not grovel or apologise for leaving. He simply stated that he would be leaving soon; that way if a suitable applicant came along, Mr Kilby could employ him and the shop would continue to run its usual smooth way. Mr Kilby admired Charlie and was not at all surprised that the boy was leaving. He had a natural authority about him. He was never obsequious but always polite. He knew the trade as well as anyone who had been in it for twenty years and Charlie was nice. Mr Kilby offered to write him a reference and decided that he would also give him a ten shilling note when he left. Now he was left with Badnell as a future manager. He was alright and had he not been taken on whilst

Charlie was on the staff, he would have seemed very good. Things would work themselves out, he decided. Things always did.

Charlie had booked his passage. He told Tom that he would be leaving in three months' time. Would he be leaving with him? Part of Tom wanted to go. He wanted to go so much. The thought of losing Charlie was almost as bad as losing Nellie. Charlie was his key to a new life. With Charlie, he felt he could do anything: ride a bicycle, learn to swim, start again in a new country, learn to read music. He wanted to do all of those things so much but he also wanted Nellie. He had to resolve matters. He felt as if his head would burst at times. So one evening, when Nellie seemed more amenable than usual, he blurted out,

"Will you marry me Nellie? We could go to Canada and start a new life together in a new country."

Nellie did not want to marry Tom, nor did she want to go to Canada. She did not even wish to set foot on a boat; even punting on the Thames seemed dangerous to her. She may have descended from Norfolk trawler men, but she knew only too well how many of them had perished at sea. The sea was lovely to sit beside and look at (she had once removed her stockings and paddled) but to sail across an ocean was not something which she even cared to contemplate, particularly in the company of Tommy Badnell.

Chapter 21

The Engagement

"If you go to Canada, I won't marry you," she said. She had unwittingly implied that if he didn't go to Canada she would and that was how he took her reply. She knew he wanted to go. She knew how much his friendship with Charlie meant so she was sure that would be an end to it. She could barely believe it when he said,

"Then I won't go Nellie. If you ever change your mind, we can follow Charlie. If not, I'm sure I'll be the next manager of the shop and I'll buy you a beautiful house."

Nellie walked home in a daze. She had gone out for a pleasant stroll, convinced that Tom would break the news to her that he, like Charlie would soon be sailing away for ever. Now here she was at only nine o'clock engaged to someone she hardly knew and he was asking if he could kiss her as they were now engaged.

"We can't be engaged until you have asked my dad," she said, and Tommy agreed to go with Nellie to Abbey Road on their next mutual day off to ask Nellie's dad for his permission to marry her. Tommy was as energetic as his room-mate. Neither of the young men let the grass grow under their feet. The next day, which was a Thursday and early closing day, the two set about putting the final touches to their separate plans. Charlie went to see the manager of the bank on the corner of Park Street and the High Street and Tommy went into Market Street to the pawnbrokers.

He had once had to redeem his sister Carrie's earrings for her from the pawnbrokers so he knew that many items were never claimed but were sold off cheaply.

Tommy explained to the old Jewish gentleman that he wanted a ring for a young lady; something pretty but not too expensive. The old man lifted out a half hoop of the most beautiful opals set with tiny diamonds. The opals themselves were small but had wonderful fire and flashed blue and green and red. Tommy had never seen anything like them. The old Jew thought that perhaps his young

116

customer might have a little Jewish blood. He had beautifully shaped hands for a country boy, although the little finger of his left hand had a strange nail which curved around like a ram's horn. He also had an elegantly curved nose, but his eyes were not Jewish, not big enough, and the lashes of a young Jew are usually long. Still, he let his customer have the ring at a good price. It was pretty but opals were said to be unlucky and were therefore hard to sell. Tommy showed Charlie his purchase and was glad that he approved. Charlie was kind enough not to mention that opals were unlucky. He only hoped that Nellie had not heard of that superstition but he somehow thought she would have.

Nellie had in fact heard of the superstition but when Tom showed her the ring, she was genuinely pleased. It really was very pretty. She could tell that it was well made and she loved the colours that flashed when she held the ring to the light. Tom had given her the ring in its little green leather box and now seeing her approval; he took it out and placed it on her ring finger.

"It could have been made for you," he said, "it fits just right; just like us, we could have been made for each other."

Nellie said nothing but went on holding her ring up to the light. It was strange but somehow the ring reminded her of Tommy; in some lights he was really quite nice, whereas in others … She gave him a little smile and said that she had not expected an engagement ring and indeed she had not for engagement rings were not always possible among poorer people.

Tommy told her that she was worth the expense; that only the best would do for her. He meant it at the time and she believed it and for a while they were happy together playing out the game of being in love, being engaged. But Tommy had been disappointed in the kiss she had given him after she put on the ring. It had far less fire than the tiny stones that she now wore on her left hand finger.

Nellie still looked for the post each morning, more out of habit now than expectation and when she cuddled her pillow at night, she still thought of John and the moment when they had found each other with their eyes on either side of the bandstand.

A few weeks after Tommy gave Nellie the opal ring, Charlie left for Canada. Tommy did not know how to feel. He had Nellie and now that they had a definite future to talk about, things were going better. He was not prepared however, for just how much he would miss Charlie. He missed the excitement which surrounded his friend; he missed having someone on whom he could completely rely, both at work and in his social life.

He went to the station to see his friend off. They still pretended that maybe one day Tommy and Nellie would join Charlie in Canada but both of them knew that in reality this was goodbye; the end of the laughs and discussions, the fun of the music halls and the larking around in rowing boats in the summer months. Charlie was supremely confident. His trunks were in the guard's van, he had letters of introduction and the bank manager had offered every help. He was off to build an empire and was Alexandrian in his confidence.

As the train drew away, both of them waved until they could no longer see each other. Tommy felt the tears running down his face for he had lost his best friend - more a father or a brother. He had lost the man who had taught him how to live and now at this time, when he needed him most, he had gone. He was on the train just disappearing from his view and he would never come back. He would build his empire and forget Maidenhead and Tommy. The dreadful thing was that Tommy could have been on that train. He could have had a ticket for Canada in his pocket but he had not and he had only himself to blame.

At that moment, if he could have stopped the train and brought it back to the station, he would have done so. He would have boarded the train and bought a ticket in Liverpool even if it was for the worst berth on the ship. For he knew then that Charlie represented the future: that bright, shiny future that took no notice of the gentry; that was prepared to challenge all that his family had always doffed their caps at. He also knew that without Charlie he would go back to nodding, agreeing and being looked down on by those, what had he called them? 'inbred idiots.'

Spontaneously, he smiled at the thought of his friend's lack of deference. He was going to miss Charlie so much, in so many ways. It was worse than when his brother had died. But then, he recalled, he had hardly known his brother.

But he had known Nellie. So he wiped his eyes, straightened his boater and went back to his digs. Tomorrow was a big day, he was going to Knowl Hill to tell his parents of his engagement. He knew his old dad would just smile and nod but his mother would be a different matter. Tommy's mother always looked at any situation from her own point of view and she would immediately want to know how she was going to benefit from this change in circumstances.

Tommy's mother was often referred to in the family as *"the old witch"*. What made matters worse for anyone living with the old witch was not just her sheer unkindness and mean spirit; it was the fact that she was a religious old witch who cited, often inaccurately and invariably inappropriately, the support of God and His Holy Bible. The God of Old Ma Badnell was not the handsome young Hebrew depicted in most Victorian churches surrounded by groups of clean and well cared for children, The God of Old Ma Badnell was a nasty, mean old Jew who would have had no time for children, lepers or the infirm. Far from casting out the money changers from the Temple, the God of the old witch would almost certainly have tried to get in on the act of usury.

Although neither Tommy nor Nellie guessed it at the time, the future relationship of Ma Badnell with the gentle Nellie could not have been worse. Nellie was naturally submissive, amiable and sweet and with a kindly mother-in-law, she would have blossomed as she was able to show friendship to almost anyone. However, it was almost impossible for anyone with a sweet and gentle nature to thrive in the face of such bullying and exploitation.

It was quite usual towards the turn of the nineteenth century for the observance of Sunday to be held as a total day of rest. It was perhaps understandable that people who laboured long and hard throughout the week should want a complete abstention from labour for one day of the week. Ma Badnell however, took things to excess. As poor Nellie was to discover in the early days of her marriage, even washing oneself was frowned upon. On seeing her young daughter-in-law emptying a basin of soapy water after washing herself one Sunday morning, the old peasant accused her of throwing dirty water in the face of the Almighty; a religious concept which even the Salvationist Nellie had never encountered before. Her religious sensibilities did not however stop her from sending out the genteel young woman to force-feed the geese in the terrifying darkness of the shed each of the seven days of the week. Strangely, had Nellie been less religious than she was, she might well have seen through the manipulative use of her mother-in-law's peculiar beliefs, but Nellie was ever eager to please and defer and besides the old witch's tempers were truly terrifying. No carefully brought up twenty year old would stand a chance against Old Ma Badnell's rages.

Tommy had duly made his way to Knowl Hill and had broken the news to his parents of his engagement to Nellie. He wanted to emphasise to his mother just how lovely his intended was: her gentility, her beauty, her lovely clothes. He should have known of course that this would not impress his mother whose face barely altered.

"Not going to Canada now then?" asked his Dad, "I'd have thought that was a good idea. I always reckoned that Charlie had his head screwed on all right. A real bright spark that Charlie, I'm glad you palled up with him."

"Charlie's gone," answered Tommy, "he'll be on the boat by now. They'll be sailing tomorrow."

Tommy's mother had been sitting still with her lips pulled tightly together so that little lines joined from all around her upper and lower lips in a tiny dark crevice. Her contribution to what passed as a conversation finished any hope of the visit being celebratory or jolly.

"Where are you going to live then? Eh? Where are you going to live with Miss High and Mighty, Posh Frocks and Fancy Hats?"

She spat out her contempt for the as yet unknown girl as though her son had met her in a bordello rather than at a totally respectable laundry.

"And what's to become of us? Don't you know in the Bible it says that children should look after their parents? Didn't they teach you anything at that Church School?"

Old Pa Badnell would have liked to have stopped her. No wonder, he thought that all his children had left and rarely returned. Ma had the knack of spoiling anything. He felt sorry for his youngest, his namesake. They were both called Richard but they had come to call the boy Tommy because of all the confusion that two Richards in the same house had caused.

It was on that fateful day Tommy recalled later, that everything had started to go wrong. His mother had shouted, sulked, reminded him of his filial duty to provide for his parents in their old age and had eventually extracted a promise from him that he would give them a home in their old age. He did not mean for several years, they were both still quite fit and the farmer had shown no sign of asking them to leave the tied cottage. If anything, he now had too many cottages for farming was becoming easier and fewer families were needed to work the land. But Tommy should have known. The old witch had her promise sworn on the Bible. A promise that Tommy, her youngest, would provide for her in her old age, as, she told him, the Bible commanded.

As the old couple saw their son off down the Lane, Tommy's mother reflected on how good the Lord was to those who helped themselves. She would not be losing a son to the snowy Canadian wastes,rather, she would be moving quite soon to a nice house in Maidenhead. Better still, she would have a young and easily dominated daughter-in-law to do all the work. She would soon be living as she had always wanted to, it would almost be as good as being one of the gentry.

As he roused himself from the memories of all those years ago, the grocer could not help a shudder on recalling the result of that day. Because of that promise, they had never stood a chance, they had both been so young. Poor Nellie, the victim of that promise to his mother; how he loathed her, wicked old witch. The kids were right, that's just what she was.

Tommy picked up his latest Western. He had been dozing again. So much had happened. Some things which he regretted might have been avoided, but other things had been beyond his control. Despite everything, they were all here together and he was glad of that. Strange things were happening in the world and then family was all that mattered.

He had so wanted a life of love and laughter but things had not panned out as he had hoped. He would always feel bad about his treatment of Nellie, she had deserved so much more, but somehow he had just never had the gift. He had never known how to show her the sort of love he had come to know that she had wanted and also deserved. Maybe if Charlie had stayed, he could have shown him?

For the art of gentle loving was something that was a luxury he decided, like knowing about wine and cigars. People like Mr Ivor Novello knew. That's why he could write those songs, songs to make your heart break. He felt a tear run down his cheek and as he rose, he wiped it away, switched off the light in the cellar and went up into the rear of the shop where the sacks of sugar, dried fruit and soda were stored.

It was not such a bad life, he reflected, as he twirled his moustache, it may well have been a lot better if he had gone to Canada, but it may also have been a lot worse. Wherever he had lived with Nellie, they would never have been suited. Perhaps another man might have made her happy: a patient, gentle man like an artist or silversmith maybe, but Nellie had never shown any interest in anyone else. He was lucky that Ada had come along and he would not have met her had he gone with Charlie. He looked down the shop with some degree of pride, for he had managed it since his early twenties and he employed a large staff and kept an excellent stock.

After checking that the doors were bolted (for the policeman would soon be round to try them at half past ten) he turned off the lights and mounted the curving stairs that led to the flat above. Nellie would soon be coming home; they may not have had the ideal marriage, but he missed her. He would be glad when she was back behind the biscuit counter and it would be nice to have thin bread and butter again. Ada was a good cook but she had never trained as a parlour maid and her bread and butter was like doorsteps. No wonder his indigestion had got worse in Nellie's absence. He put on the stair light and straightened the little pots of Capstan and Shippam's paste on the corner shelves to the right of the stairs and finally went upstairs to bed.

Chapter 22

The Homecoming

The entire family made a great effort to welcome Nellie back after her time with Old Walter. Ada, with a very little help from Kathleen, had spring cleaned the flat and with the artistic flair which she had inherited from her mother Kathleen decorated every table and mantelpiece with fresh flowers. Sunday tea was even more lavish than usual and there was a bright fire in the grate.

Phil had been working on a surprise for his mother and had managed to finish a wireless that he had made from a kit. Nellie could not quite understand his explanation of how it worked. She presumed it just made the voices of the people in London very loud and squeezed them down a tube; rather in the way that people had very hot water in a tank and by the time it got to the tap it was the right temperature. But she didn't care how it worked, she was so proud of Phil and that he had managed to make it.

Nellie actually felt a real sense of homecoming as she was settled into the chair by the fire. Even Lupa the little dog came from under the table and wagged his tail. He really was a dear little dog and very good, ideal in fact for them. He seemed to live quite happily in his basket under the table, only emerging to welcome members of the family as they returned from work or from downstairs in the shop each evening. Nellie knelt to pat the small creature who was wriggling with joyful recognition. She had always thought of him as Tom's dog, for Tom in fact had nearly managed to start a new breed called 'Lupa' dogs. But now she realised that the dog recognised her and it gave her a great surge of pleasure. Even more pleasurable was feeling Kathleen's arm around her shoulder as she perched on the narrow arm of the chair and said, "I'm glad you're back Mum," and kissed her on the top of her head.

Kathleen had started work and was full of her job in Bond Street. Nellie could hardly believe that here she was wearing a sapphire ring from Biggs and listening to her daughter telling her about going to

Kensington Palace with Miss Jevons to photograph the Spanish royal family. None of the family could really believe it.

"And would you believe it?" she was saying, "We put in all the light bulbs to photograph them and blew the whole electric system in the palace."

The older members of the family were quite shocked that this could have occurred. When Nellie enquired if this had caused an awful lot of trouble, Kathleen blithely replied that no, Miss Jevons had just sent her back to Bond Street in a taxi to pick up even more light bulbs and the palace had apparently managed to get an electrician to mend their electricity system and the photographic session had gone ahead.

"I wonder they didn't kick you all out, wrecking their palace," commented Ada, "you should have more respect."

But the young woman laughed and said, "Well if they want to be photographed for posterity by the top London photographer the very least they could have done was provide an electricity system capable of taking more than a couple of light bulbs. Honestly Miss Jevons said it's medieval that palace, medieval."

None of the adults knew what medieval meant so Tommy said somewhat brusquely, "I think we've had enough of Miss Jevons and do remember your mother is not to be tired Kathleen." He picked up his copy of '*Blazing Wagons*' and dropped out of the conversation.

Previously this would have been the signal for everyone else in the family to fall silent, but Kathleen was surprisingly delighted to have her mother home. She had already shared the amusing experiences of the last few weeks with her auntie and now she wanted to tell her mother as she knew it would amuse her. Nellie looked across at her daughter and gave a little conspiratorial smile so Kathleen continued,

"And then, you'll never guess what Miss Jevons said."

"No, I won't," said Tom, "so I'll go down and do a bit of book keeping." He picked up his book and his snuff box and leaving his chair by the fire, he took his jacket from behind the door and went out onto the tiny landing.

When they heard the light click on and his footsteps on the stairs, Kathleen said, "Well at least now he's gone we can all feel the fire and say what we want."

124

Nellie and Ada went to reprimand her but then both laughed. She was right. They had a right to talk, laugh and feel the fire.

"Well," said Kathleen, "as I was saying before I was so rudely interrupted by my dear father, when I got back to the palace in the taxi, they had got Queen Ena and all the grown-ups all organised - and by the way Miss Jevons says those pearls are not genuine – either the real ones were left in Spain, or perhaps they are in hock!" She roared with laughter and after a while the two older women joined in. They may not have been deferential in the way that Tommy was to royalty, but they really thought that Kathleen should show a little more respect. Nonetheless it was quite amusing.

Kathleen was well into her story now, "…and then Mum you will never guess what happened! Well, the baby, Juan something or other (nice little baby) well he would keep crawling all over the place and Miss Jevons threw me her fox fur and said: 'Miss Badnell, please will you get down on the floor and play with the future King of Spain? That's how we refer to him: not as 'the baby', as 'the future King of Spain'."

The two older women were quite literally open-mouthed.

"You mean you have touched royalty?" said Ada, "actually touched a future king?"

"Of course," answered her niece, "you can't really play with a baby without touching him now can you?"

The two older women hardly knew what to say. They had seen Queen Mary of course when she came to Biggs across the road. Then they stood on the balcony outside the front parlour and looked at the Queen's arrival in silent awe. Tommy would stand outside the shop door, raise his boater and call out, "God bless you Ma'am, God Bless you." He always (to Kathleen's embarrassment) pronounced God as 'Gawd' and he always came in from his patriotic ritual with tears streaming down his face which the older members of the shop staff found touching but the younger errand boys found hilarious. They were sensible enough to keep their hilarity to themselves.

But to be in the same room as royalty (five generations Kathleen had said) to see them close to, to touch a prince, a future king, even if the poor child was the future King of Spain; their amazement and their admiration for young Kathleen knew no bounds. To think how far they had come, it seemed such a short while ago that they were

125

eating bread and dripping under the table and now Kathleen was taking taxis between Bond Street and Kensington Palace, life was truly surprising. Nellie knew that this was her sign. Of course she was meant to come home, she was a lucky woman. She had a warm cosy home, a son who had made her a wireless, a dog who had recognised her and a daughter who had played with the future King of Spain.

At exactly ten o'clock, Nellie and Ada had their cup of hot water. They had both put on a little weight and hot water was said to be good for the waist line. They filled their hot water bottles from the same kettle, it was so nice to get into a nice cosy bed. Tommy would put Lupa out into the yard before he came up to bed, just as he would wind the clock and check the doors and windows. They kissed each other goodnight on the tiny upper landing and Nellie went into the large front bedroom, undressed and sat at the dressing table. She rubbed her hair with a silk scarf, rubbed Ponds cold cream onto her face and wiped it off with a piece of cotton wool. Then she got into her side of the big bed with the thick feather mattress. At half past ten, her husband joined her in the bedroom. After he had undressed, he knelt and said his prayers at the side of the bed, as he always did, and then climbed into the right-hand side of the bed. She had an awful moment of dread as he leant over her, but he kissed her on the cheek as he had done at her father's house and said, "Goodnight Nellie, I'm so glad you've come home."

Nellie pulled the cord above the bed and turned off the light. She hoped that Tom would not snore too loudly, but apart from that she was very happy to be home.

Chapter 23

Storm Clouds

Young Kathleen's story of the little future King of Spain reminded the family that whilst things were, as ever, going well in their tiny world of Maidenhead, in other parts of the world (and indeed in other parts of the country) things were far from fine and dandy.

Tom read the Express each day and this was sounding warnings about a man called Hitler and in Tommy's favourite country a man called Mussolini had come to power. Some people said he was just what the Ities needed: made them run their trains on time and was making them pull their socks up. Tommy didn't contradict them but he knew Italy and the Italians. They were not lazy. Some of the people sounding off in the shop should try working in that heat; they should try making crops grow in that thin soil. He felt his eyes moistening and said,

"It's them Gerries, that's who we need to look out for. It's always Gerry that's the root of the problem."

Everyone agreed.

Maidenhead had many refugees. In the twenties, several Russian ladies lived in the homes of wealthy friends down by the river. One had become very friendly with Nellie. She was lonely and bored and asked 'the grocer's sweet wife' to play cards with her on early closing day. Nellie was such a poor card player that the Russian lady said after the first hand that they could not play for money, Nellie hadn't realised that they had been. It would be like taking sweeties from children, she had said, and for once she had laughed with real merriment.

The arrangement continued for some months until one day the Russian lady said, "Dear Nellie, sweet Mrs Badnell, once again I am having to leave, the storm clouds are gathering again I fear. I am Russian. I can feel it in my bones. This Hitler and his friend: this Mussolini, they will tear Europe apart. For you it is alright my

Nellie. You are British and I tell you Nellie you have drawn first prize in God's lottery."

Nellie felt very confused.

"You'll be alright here," she said, "everyone is alright in Maidenhead. You'll see."

Her card-playing friend pulled a leather jewel case from under a settee and said, "Now my Nellie you have been the only friend that I have had in this place, I think you are a very sweet lady. Yes, you are a true lady and I should know."

She opened the lid of the box and insisted, "Now choose, Nellie. Choose something to remember your Old Russian Duchess."

Nellie genuinely thought that she would faint. Not only did the box look as though it was full of the most incredible jewels, the lady holding it open and insisting that she choose (just as her other friends would insist that she choose a chocolate) seemed to be a Duchess; a Russian Duchess. Spanish kings and now Russian Duchesses; where would it all end?

Nellie picked her way through the jewels. She was hoping there would be a small silver chain or a tiny pearl brooch but the smallest thing that she could find was a little gold cross. It was very dirty and failed to sparkle so she assumed it could not be worth much.

"I think I should like this," she said.

"You have chosen well," smiled her friend, "It is Byzantine; very beautiful. Take care of it and remember your old Russian friend and remember that not all Russians are Bolsheviks." She embraced the pretty grocer's wife in a way that Nellie found quite disturbing (foreigners were so dramatic) but she kissed the old woman on the cheek and wished her a safe journey to wherever she was going. She was quite glad to get out of the flat and into the fresh air. She walked back from the river, past the moor, over the colonnade and up the High Street. She couldn't resist a look in Biggs but there was nothing like her cross in the window.

When she got home, she sat at her dressing table and held the cross up to the light but it failed to sparkle at all. When she showed it to Ada, her sister commented that if she wore it people would take her for a catholic. So Nellie put it at the back of the left hand drawer of her dressing table and there is lay for the next thirty years along with the small opal ring that she had liked so much until her bitter and spiteful mother-in-law had told her how unlucky opals were. Nellie forgot about the jewels and they gathered layers of face powder and dust but she remembered the Old Russian Duchess and worried about her. If only she had stayed in Maidenhead, they could have kept her safe, Nellie was certain of that.

There were soon other things to worry about. The people in the north of the country were out of work and demanding that the government do something and Old Walter agreed with them. Tommy decided that he did his bit by being Father Christmas each year and indeed he did do his bit. Each year the preparations started earlier and the presents became more lavish. Each year someone had the temerity to suggest that Tommy buy a small gift for the men, but each year he adamantly refused. Ada even suggested that they could be given a piece of soap or a packet of razor blades but Tommy made it quite clear that he was against giving the men anything on principle.

It was strange because in his own way he had enormous sympathy with people who were the underdog. If a gypsy should come into the shop selling lavender or heather, he always made a purchase. If someone of Jewish race came into the shop he burst into,

'Only a Jew, but an insult I'll remember,
Only a Jew, then why not Christian too?'

His appalling ability to have a song for every occasion caused a great deal of embarrassment to everyone but he seemed blissfully unaware of how offensive he was, cheerfully greeting the very rare black person he met with,

"Hello Sambo" and speaking to them as if they had just escaped from the plantation. Tommy knew all about the slave trade, lynch mobs and the dreadful treatment handed out to the black people in America. Charlie still wrote often and sent him magazines and papers so Tommy knew.

Tommy felt a real sense of camaraderie with the poor and oppressed. He may, by this time, have owned several houses; he may have gravel pits and a funeral and carting business, but in his own eyes he had far more in common with an escaped slave from the plantation than he did with all of the writers and actors who lived near the river and who were far poorer financially than he.

His sense of one with the poor and oppressed however, never extended to the men of the Barracks. He always felt that they had done little to improve their own lot and had failed to provide, as he had, for their wives and children. Tommy had good reason to be pleased with himself when he considered his early years in Knowl Hill and his mother's expectation that he should spend his life as a ploughman. He had done well to amass property and money and to directly and indirectly provide for so many friends and relatives. True, whenever the eagerly awaited letters arrived from Canada, Tommy felt he could have achieved more. He and Charlie were always a great team and he knew that Charlie had always had the ability to bring out the best in him. Charlie was always the man to live up to. Perhaps, he thought in a rare moment of self-knowledge, jealousy may have crept in, but he somehow doubted this for he had always deferred to Charlie because Charlie was what he wanted to be: confident, smart, well-spoken and respected by everyone. There was no doubt about it; Charlie had left him too early, before his education was finished. Had his friend stayed, he would have gone to concerts, learnt more about politics and other countries. But Charlie had not stayed. He had seized the moment, gone to the place of the future and set about building his dream.

Now Charlie's dream had almost come true. He already had several stores across Canada and was starting to mention something called 'supermarkets' in his letters. These were stores where the customers helped themselves and paid as they went out. Tommy discussed this phenomenon with Nellie. Both decided that controlling pilfering and stealing would be impossible,

"Asking for trouble," was Tommy's opinion, "putting temptation in people's way; that's why you have counters, to keep the goods from the customers and so they only buy what they want."

"Of course," said Nellie thoughtfully, "but if they were to buy more than they wanted and you could make them pay for it all, then I suppose your profits could only go up."

This piece of marketing strategy seemed so radical to Tommy that he was hard pressed to find an answer so he came out with a standard reply, "You may well be right my dear, you may well be right. But it would never catch on here, not in Maidenhead." He thought this would be an end to the discussion but Nellie came back to him with,

"Next time you write to Charlie, ask him how they get people to pay for the goods and how they keep on top of the pilfering." Nellie was fairly certain that if Charlie was pursuing an idea there must be something in it and secretly Tommy thought she might have a point.

Charlie's letters were full of how Canada was developing; people were flocking there from all over Europe. It was still a land of opportunity he said and he was so glad that he had gone there in the early days; glad that he had seen the mountains and rivers, seen the dams built by creatures called beavers and watched the salmon leaping in the clear rushing rivers. Tommy would have liked to see the salmon leaping too. Charlie, it seemed, had gone to New York to see a supermarket. He seemed to travel a great deal and Nellie thought that reading between the lines, Charlie was even more successful than he was letting on.

After each letter arrived, Tommy would sit down at the table with his Basildon Bond writing paper and envelopes, his orange and black Watermans fountain pen with his signature raised on the side and his bottle of Parker ink. Nellie would lay it all out for him on a piece of pink blotting paper; rather as a theatre nurse lays out surgical instruments for a surgeon. Then slowly, having taken off his starched collar and his jacket, Tommy would begin the laborious and creative process of writing, or possibly in his case, 'wrighting' a letter to his friend. Once he had decided on what he wanted to say, he rarely paused. The beautiful copperplate handwriting flowed across the blue paper letting Charlie know of all the family's successes and a few of the happenings in the town such as who had died or retired or married. Tommy never had need of a dictionary; he seemed blessed with faultless spelling although he had left school at twelve to become a ploughboy. When the letter was finished, he would seal the envelope, put on the stamp and leave the rest to Nellie.

"There you are, Nellie," he would say, "That can go to the post tomorrow."

It always did.

Chapter 24

The Silver Wedding

A sort of frenzied excitement would come over the whole shop near to Christmas. There was of course endless work making up orders, wrapping and tucking and heaving out the heavy crates of empty soda syphons when they were brought in to be exchanged for full ones.

"Heavens alone knows how many whiskies and soda's must be drunk in this town each night," Ada once remarked. But Tommy said not to discourage them; their own comfortable retirement depended on people drinking themselves silly. He added when he saw her look of disapproval, "Anyway it's Christmas and it's only once a year!"

The preparations for the Christmas gifts started very early. Toward the middle of October, Tommy would have the raffle books printed and usually an Olde Tyme Dance, a concert, or sometimes both were planned.

Tommy liked to do things in style and when he gave his Olde Tyme Dances, the ladies were all given little dance cards in which to write the names of their partners for the various dances which were also listed. The dance cards were printed in just the way that a grand Victorian hostess would have had them printed: stiff cream-coloured card was cut with crinkled edges and bordered with gold and violet or gold with pink or turquoise and a small pencil in the same shade was attached with a matching cord. Everything was very stylish, copying exactly the grand style of the Edwardian gentry who Tommy admired so much and wished to emulate. The occasion of Tommy and Nellie's silver wedding demonstrated just how well Tommy was able to do things.

Tommy may well have retained many of the less fortunate habits of his early life, but he was a quick learner. He observed, watched and was always fascinated by the ease and grace with which the upper classes moved through their lives. He loved the smooth faces of the ladies, their soft hands usually covered with tight kid gloves but sometimes uncovered to reveal the rings which demonstrated their own glittering position in society. Tommy liked the way the gentlemen spoke; the casualness with which they told the world that there was no stress in their lives, no worries about bills or failing businesses. God had put them on the earth to grace it, to give instructions to lesser mortals and if danger should strike the nation, then these were the men to send others in to battle, to give orders and ultimately to receive the accolades for victory. It may all be very unfair, but Tommy did not see it that way. Like most men of his time and class, he accepted the differences which birth bestowed. For much of the time he admired these natural leaders and whilst he knew that he would never join their ranks, he hoped that one day one of his heirs might take their own place in the sun; perhaps in a grand house by the river in Maidenhead or Henley. True, he had resented some of the officers under whom he had served in the war, but most of them were not proper gentry, they were jumped up sons of tradesmen who had gone to the grammar school, just as his Phil did. But by and large, Tommy was happy with his place in the scheme of things. True, he wanted to go higher and better or as he often quoted from his favourite poem, Excelsior, Excelsior! For now he was happy to copy the ways of the privileged by careful imitation.

His silver wedding was just the opportunity he needed to show the rest of Maidenhead how clever he was at putting on a grand show. No expense would be spared; it would be a glittering occasion. People would talk of it for months after the event and in this matter at least, he was right. People did speak of the Badnell's Silver Wedding for months, if not years after the event; but it was not only the little dance cards and the cascading silver stars that stayed in their memories – more is the pity.

Tommy was a natural dancer Ada thought as she looked down from the gallery at the Pearce Hall. Tom had always been good at physical things, he was good with horses and dogs and he seemed to have a natural sort of rhythm that helped him to dance with ease and surprising grace. Like any natural dancer, Tom liked to have a good partner. To his disappointment on the dance floor, just as in the marriage bed, Nellie was not his equal; she was just too stiff, she didn't let herself go. She always looked as if she disapproved of the whole occasion and whilst she certainly smiled and looked sweet, she was uncomfortable and ill at ease.

The committee of the Olde Tyme Dances had planned a wonderful surprise for Tommy and Nellie. There was to be a grand parade with Tommy leading his wife down the centre of the hall and everyone following, relatives taking precedence, other civic notables and then friends and other guests. The surprise was that as the procession came to an end, dozens of little umbrellas suspended above the hall would open and cascades of silver stars would shower the couple, their family and friends with sparkling sequins. At that point, a committee member would mount the stage and make a speech on the subject of love, marriage, the family and what an example of all three Tommy, his wife and family offered.

The parade took place and as the silver stars cascaded, sighs of ooh and ah arose; what style, what extravagance! People said that even at Cliveden they would be hard pressed to put on such a show. As the music for the parade ended and the designated committee member was making his way to the stage to voice his well-prepared speech of congratulations, most of the couples turned to one another and smiled or laughed at the pleasure of the event. But Tommy, seeing his favourite dancing partner sitting alone for some reason, made his way towards her. He could hear the band starting to play, very softly in fact as an interlude before the planned speech, his favourite dance which was the waltz. Quickly, pulling the startled lady to her feet, he started to whirl her around the floor, oblivious to the fact that the entire company who were awaiting the presentation were sharing in the awkwardness of the gentleman on the stage. He who had thought he would be addressing a devoted couple standing together at the high point of their marriage, now looked down on a distressed lady standing alone whilst her husband glided, with obvious enjoyment, around the room with someone else.

Nellie could feel the sympathy sticking to her along with the silver stars. It had the feel of treacle: sweet, uncomfortable and very undesirable. By the time that Tommy had been summoned to the spotlight, Nellie had made her way to her table at the side of the hall and no pleading could persuade her to leave it for the rest of the evening. As usual, Tommy seemed unaware of the anguish he had caused, accepting the good wishes of the company with a total lack of embarrassment.

Ada looked down from the gallery and shared her sister's unhappiness. Of all the men who had perished in the war, she sometimes asked herself why Tommy Badnell had to be one of those who were spared. The war years had been good; she and Nellie together with Phil, Mona, Gladys and young Kath. Tom would never change. He was selfish, unfeeling and totally unaware of what unhappiness he caused. But it was too late now. The courses of their lives were irrevocably set.

She got up and started on the walk back to the shop. Someone had to see to the dog, the fire and the kettle; they would all want a drink when they got in. She liked having the flat to herself, it happened so rarely. She made a cup of tea and sat, where she always did, in the chair by the big roll top desk and mused about the past. There were parts that she had tucked away so carefully to the back of her memory that it was almost impossible to recall all of them and that was how she liked it. Some things were too painful: seeing pianos crashing past the window; hearing the crowd baying for blood and the cries of "Jew, Jew, Jew." She finished her tea and pulled down the blinds on that hidden part of her memory. She was in Maidenhead now, not the East End. She was safe and comfortable and her brother-in-law might be a thoughtless pig, but in his own way he did love her. She had her own plans for her future which involved a lovely house within walking distance of the High Street. Like Nellie, she kept quiet about it. She was very good at keeping quiet about much of her life. No-one ever questioned why she always had nice clothes, always had money in her purse. Did they ever wonder or did they simply not want to know. Either way it suited her. There were certain things that she had promised she would never tell and she never would.

There had been an occasion when she thought her secrets might be discovered; a day which had begun much like many other days when Nellie had sent a message up the stairs that a lady (she had emphasised the word 'lady') was here in the shop to see Ada. Ada, logically thinking that there was a discrepancy in a bill, had started to come down the stairs with her ledger in her hand but as she rounded the bend of the staircase, before she was visible to anyone in the shop, she spotted her. She hadn't changed a lot, still the same soft, well cared for look, the same beautiful clothes, and this time in deep violet. She had seen her years ago, the favoured one - the one chosen by the family. It was no use that she had his promise, she had his child - that had counted for nothing with his family. She looked at the soft violet mourning clothes. He must have

135

died. The father of her children and she had been given no chance to say goodbye.

The sense of this new loss, of all the other losses, the betrayal and the deep-seated loneliness washed over Ada like a blizzard. All at once the wretchedness she had smothered for so long rose in her throat and threatened to spew down the dark stairs which she had descended in such a carefree and everyday manner just a few seconds before.

As soon as she reached the tiny landing, she put her arm around the door and lifted down her coat. At the bottom of the stairs she turned left, through the gap between the counter and the bacon slicer, out of the back door, around the side of the slaughter-house and out into the High Street. Ada walked in the way that only the desperate can. She turned left into Queen Street, left towards the station, under the railway arch and off up the Braywick Road. It seemed she never drew breath. As long as she was walking, walking, walking as if all the demons of Hell were at her heels, she could stop the tears. She could stop the nausea that welled up inside her and threatened to displace the control and resignation she had maintained for so long.

She had tried to hate him, tried to see how weak and unfaithful he had been to her and to their children, but the fact remained that she had loved him and would have done anything to have held him to her once more before he had died – sent a message even, told him about little Gladys. By the time she got to the fork in the road where the left road leads off to Windsor and the right to Holyport and the other woolly-back country villages, she had to stop and catch her breath. She crashed more than leant against the red brick wall that had managed to hold some warmth from the morning sunshine. The moment that she stopped walking, the tears came. At first they started to trickle and then like a river in full spate, they came faster and stronger until they wracked her whole body shaking her against the wall and dislodging all the long-held emotions and hidden sorrows which she had concealed so carefully for so long. She had no idea how long she was there, how long she howled and shook, oblivious of passers-by. When things were starting to subside, just as she was searching in her pockets for a handkerchief or scarf to wipe her face, a country woman came past and putting her arm around her she asked what the matter was. Ada replied without thinking and quite truthfully in her eyes that she had just lost her husband. The woman gave her a look of great sympathy and asked her where she lived

136

and on hearing that Maidenhead was her address, she said that she was going there and would walk along with her. She was the ideal companion, for being a widow herself she knew that no words were necessary, but that the presence of another human was a great comfort.

Nellie had the table ready when Ada got in. Nothing was said, but Nellie handed her sister the note which the unknown lady had given into her keeping. Nellie knew instinctively that this was part of her sister's life that must remain secret, out of bounds, part of the sadness she kept hidden away like a damaged but once beautiful petticoat, past repair but too precious to discard.

Sometime later, following the instructions in the envelope that her sister had handed her, Ada visited the same bank her brother-in-law used and a short while after that she put down a deposit on a house in St Luke's Road. She also purchased some sovereigns which she kept in a stocking under the mattress. Someone did once question where the money had come from and she replied with no hesitation that it had come from her husband. No more was said about the visitor in mourning clothes, nor was Ada ever questioned as to how she had money for pictures, clothes or treats for the children for the duration of her life. There had been too much sorrow. Like Nellie, Ada would love their children and make the most of their lives together. There really was no alternative.

Shortly after midnight on the night of their Silver Wedding party, Tommy and Nellie left the Pearce Hall and started the short walk back to the High Street. Tommy was ecstatic about the event, how good the band had been and what lavish presents they had been given. They managed to share a joke on the way home about the way that Mrs Day, the wife of Billy Day the decorator, had been turned out. They really were a most amusing looking couple: he so small and she so large and imposing, dressed as she often was in a garment which she had managed to concoct from pieces of other gowns. Mrs Day wore these creations with great panache, quite oblivious to the fact that the stitches often showed and that she and her diminutive husband looked as if they had just stepped from the picture of a saucy seaside postcard. Tommy started to sing,

'After the ball was over,
After the ball was done,
After the ball was over,

After the stars had gone ...'
He was still singing the song as he and Nellie arrived back at the flat. Ada caught her sister's eye and the two of them exchanged a wry smile. Tommy was quite immune to the irony of the words as the two of them joined in the last couplet,
'Many a heart will be broken,
After the ball.'
He was so pleased that they had joined in; it showed that they were enjoying themselves. He looked at them, his two lovely girls and broke into his favourite song,
'Two little girls in blue lad,
Two little girls in blue,
They were sisters, we were brothers,
We learnt to love the two.
Now one little girl in blue lad,
Won your father's heart,
She became your mother, I married the other,
And now we have drifted apart.'
He gave them both a large, beery kiss on the cheek and made for the stairs, humming to himself. Soon the two women followed him.

Privately, each one as they undressed and got into bed, thought that the day had been a success. Tommy reflected on how well he had danced and what a good show they had put on. Nellie thought how nice the silver tea service would look in the display cabinet in the front parlour and Ada thought she was pleased that they could all have a lie in the next morning and for once it surely wouldn't matter if they didn't get to church on time.

Ada could hear her brother-in-law humming away to himself for quite some time; he had changed tune and was singing,
'Just like the ivy, I'll cling to you.'
Ada thought wryly that she hoped Tom wasn't thinking of clinging to his wife, for that would certainly spoil Nellie's Silver Wedding celebrations.

Chapter 25

The Secrets

It was strange that Nellie had secrets of her own, just as Ada had. No-one really knew, or ever was to know, the secrets of Ada's lost years; they could only be guessed at. Nellie's secrets were different for there was no disgrace attached to either. There was the secret of the house that she kept for several years although there was no scandal involved in owning a property, or in the manner she had come by it. But her other secret was one she kept jealously to herself and shared with no-one and it was only suspected in her old age by her daughter and grand-daughter. The secret, which none of her friends or relatives would have dreamed of (and her husband would have laughed at) was a man, a very young man called John.

John was the man who would have made Nellie happy. John was young, kind and loving. He was also the only man with whom Nellie ever fell in love. She had loved John with no reservations. She could have fallen willingly into his arms each night and awoken with joy each morning at the thought of seeing his face. John had the wonderful quality of being eternally young for he had died at the age of twenty-one; crushed after a few moments of panic against a pillar holding up the pier. In one of the last desperate moments of his life, when excitement and thrill had turned with a freak wave into danger and pain, he had thought of the beautiful girl he was to marry. But the thought was a brief one for he was picked up and smashed against the mussel-strewn pillar like a bottle and was as easily crushed.

His friends could not believe the accident. It was a freak; one of those calamities which happens each year at the seaside. But it was a shame that it was John. They all agreed that he was one of the best, one of nature's gentlemen and he had met that nice girl at the bandstand. He had said one day he was going to marry her.

They let his mother know. She was so stunned with grief that for a while she could do nothing, but when John's landlady had asked

139

yet again if she could come to collect his effects, she went and found the letters.

It was reading the letters that was the start of the healing. Reading of the love the two young people had shared, the mother knew at least (if only briefly) that her son had experienced life's greatest emotion. He had loved and been loved. She had written to Nellie, said she would like to meet her, that there would always be a home with John's family if ever she needed one. Nellie did not reply as she might have done three months earlier, for the letter arrived on the eve of her wedding to Tom.

Nellie had opened the unfamiliar envelope. Her spirits were low already as her parents would not give their blessing to the union and refused to attend the wedding. She had no idea of where her sister Ada was. The only people who seemed in favour of the match were Tom, his family and her aunt who was giving her the magnificent dress in which she had been married herself.

Brides often feel faint but after reading the letter Nellie passed right out. There were just so many emotions swirling around, she seemed unable to stay conscious and when she did, she vomited violently. Her aunt, with whom she was living, was at her wits end as to what to do with her; everything was arranged, everything planned. She thought at first when she heard Nellie calling, "It's John. On no, not John," that Nellie's former sweetheart had turned up to claim her. But no, it seemed that the poor boy had died in a freak swimming accident.

These things happened all the time but why had they told the poor girl today? Could they not have kept the dreadful event a secret? What possible good could come of telling Nellie of the young man's tragic end? And today! Well, at least he wouldn't be turning up to say there was a let or hindrance now, would he? She had a terrible feeling that her niece had hoped that might happen. Everyone had someone extra special in their lives and very few were lucky enough to marry that special person. She took a deep breath and set her face. She had to get Nellie to the church. Thank goodness the dress was deep pink: blotting paper pink overlaid with cream lace; the pink would give her a bit of colour. If only she would stop crying for a few minutes she would still make a lovely bride. But Nellie was inconsolable. Although the marriage went ahead, she cried all the way to the church and went through the service like an automaton.

Nellie stored the memory of the beautiful young swimmer away in her heart and in time distilled his memory into one of utter perfection. John, who had been laughing, full of life and love to within moments of his death, was caught like a glorious dragonfly in the amber of Nellie's memory. He was her treasure, her secret friend and lover. As the years went by, their love grew and those who knew her well learnt to recognise her secret smile, it was one that she sometimes gave to him.

Nellie's time in hospital had given them a time of peace together. It was a time for Nellie to consolidate the love she had always known was there. Now she felt she could face the world, cope with the weak and selfish man she had married, for she still had her love and he would be with her for eternity.

Chapter 26

Dreams End

Despite Tommy showing himself up at the silver wedding and despite the fact that people whispered about his domestic arrangements, his annual visits to the Barracks each Christmas brought Maidenhead's Santa considerable good will in the town. The more cultured members of the town may have looked skywards at the thought of his concerts, but they were greatly enjoyed by many people who welcomed a good night out and an excuse to dress up and be seen by their neighbours. The chances of him becoming mayor were starting to look quite promising by the middle of the nineteen thirties yet somehow the prize always managed to elude him.

Although he had moved on so far from his origins in Knowl Hill and although he was a man of considerable property, he did not seem to come over as mayor material to the people who mattered. Perhaps one of his problems was his temper. Tommy had the sort of temper that was much like a sneeze. When his temper flashed nothing on earth could stop it. True it was over in a blink, but often so much damage was done in that brief moment that it was impossible to put things right when calm had replaced the surge of anger. Perhaps if his friendship with Charlie had lasted longer and had he had more time to watch and listen to that calm, kind and successful young man, then he might well have achieved more of his aims in life. As it was his temper was like a ferret; always waiting just inside his waistcoat to pop out and bite someone. It might disappear just as quickly, but the damage would be done; people would shy away at the sheer viciousness and unpredictability of the creature.

One occasion finally ended all his chances of civic glory. Tommy sat on the chamber of commerce, a group of the great and the good in the borough's trading community. The discussion was whether or not to have Wednesday or Thursday as early closing day. Most people were of the opinion that as most of the neighbouring towns had

Wednesday as their half day, Maidenhead would benefit from taking Thursday. In that way, it should gain from a good trading day on Wednesdays when the other towns were closed in the afternoons. Of course Tommy could see this argument but he did not want to agree. Doreen, his favourite assistant had a very good reason for wanting to close on Wednesday; her sweetheart worked in Windsor and as a result they had very little time together. On the strength of this alone, Tommy argued fiercely for Wednesdays. He was almost the only person who did. He could not understand how unreasonable they could be, he could see poor little Doreen's face, and now he would have to tell her that he had let her down. She would look sad and say how unfair it all was. Unfair. Like the curry combs; people were always pushing others around. The ferret was jumping out of his waistcoat. He was standing up and shouting,

"If that's what you think, well flick you, flick the flippin' lot of you, and you know what you can do with your flippin' Chamber of Commerce." And he was away down the stairs of the town hall; already regretting by the time he had reached the High Street that he had dashed all his dreams of advancement by himself.

As the wave of anger subsided and the ferret temper sank out of sight, he thought he could hear Charlie saying, *'Perhaps Gentlemen, although I am forced to agree with you at this time, we could leave the issue open to revue.'*

Everyone would have thought how wise and dignified he was. Next year they would have agreed to a trial run of Wednesday early closing, the year after they may well have voted him mayor for his charity work; but now they would not. Because he wasn't Charlie, he was still Tommy from Knowl Hill. If the family was ever going to make it then it was up to Phil or Kath, and heaven alone knew what hoity-toity ideas she was getting in Bond Street.

Kathleen was full of gossip and there was a great deal of it from 1936 onwards. The old king: King George the Fifth had died and with him the last of the old ideas of monarchy. His son, George the Sixth, was also loved but the old King held all the aura of majesty from the days when monarchs were remote and aloof; when they still held the last vestiges of divinity which kept their people in awe and wonder, as well as devotion and affection. King George and Queen Mary were king and queen and emperor and empress as well. They presided over the vast area coloured red in the atlas. The cloak of divinity which covered their shoulders was never again to shelter a British monarch from criticism and attack. An American divorcee called Wallis Simpson was to see to that.

By the morning after the old King's death, every shop window in Maidenhead was stripped of goods and was draped in mourning black. With no directive from politicians or clergymen, the people of every town and parish in the land knew what was expected of them. They knew what was the right and proper thing to do, and they did it. The town wore an air of total sobriety. Each citizen felt the loss of the king who had led them for so long and every man wore a black arm-band showing his sense of loyalty, patriotism and loss.

King George and Queen Mary; their portraits had been hung in almost every shop and home in the country and now the king was dead and at a time when the storm clouds were gathering over Europe once again. Those who had fought in the Great War could feel it coming: a sense of foreboding. But the young ones talked of the Prince of Wales, they sang the songs of Noël Coward and enjoyed a way of life and freedoms only dreamed of by their parents.

Young Kathleen became one of the first women in the town to own and drive a car. Phil had managed to get her a little MG sports car and she and Maurice were always off somewhere in it. Kathleen wore a white leather helmet and looked quite the part. Tommy worried about what they might be up to but Ada said they had eyes for no-one but each other so did it really matter? Phil had also found his great love quickly and locally. He and Bill's daughter had decided in their early teens that there was no-one else for either of them and indeed they remained devoted for the rest of their lives.

The Pragnells, Bill's family, were a jolly and practical lot and their sense of fun lightened the lives of the Badnells. The Pragnells had parties and a gramophone. They would push back the furniture at the drop of a hat and dance and sing. The young people were all pairing up and a jolly lot they were, but Kathleen was one of the prettiest and the most talented of them all.

Tommy would never let anyone know, but secretly he had to admire the girl. Her young man might well be barmy but he was good looking and his violin playing gave the concerts at the town hall quite a classy touch. Tommy hoped he might get the boy's mother to sing one day; apparently she had one of the most beautiful contralto voices in the county. He wasn't sure what that meant, but one of his customers had told him that she had once heard Elsie sing and as the customer was wearing a very nice mink coat, he was sure she knew what she was talking about.

Next year, 1938, Kathleen would be twenty-one. He supposed she would be getting married to her young man. He was training to be an accountant so perhaps he wasn't as barmy as he sometimes seemed with his soft blonde hair, his pale blue velvet trousers and his violin playing. When he had pointed out to Nellie that the young man wore strange clothes, she smiled and said that Maurice was a Bohemian and now that Kathleen had taken up Grecian dancing like Isadora Duncan, she supposed that Kathleen was a Bohemian too.

Tommy hadn't a clue what they were talking about. They were always talking about things he knew nothing of. More and more he realised that the women (and Kathleen was now one too) hid their secrets from him. They had little jokes and plans he knew nothing of. Kathleen was starting to take some very good photographs. She had taken one of him; he looked very distinguished, wearing his hat to cover his baldness and holding his silver banded walking stick. That was as he saw himself, a man of property; respected and looked up to. He really liked that photograph. When he had questioned her about the unfamiliar signature in the corner of the picture, Kathleen had replied that Karen Howard was her professional name. Tommy could not understand why her own name wasn't good enough. He had chosen Kathleen after the song, *'I'll take you home again Kathleen.'* He didn't like the name Karen, it sounded foreign. He thought Kathleen was a pretty name but his daughter said it sounded as though she was an Irish colleen fleeing from the potato famine. It was not very 'Bond Street.'

In London, his daughter's friends called her Kate or Katy and sometimes for some strange reason, Micky. They all had silly names like Jonah, Tony and Dickie. Thank goodness that at least one was called Norah; that at least sounded normal.

Chapter 27

The Magnificent Umbrella

Tommy of course had Christmas to see to before his daughter's twenty-first birthday in January but he did think that he should book the drill hall and hire a band. He would put on a good show: caterers and flowers; he would invite all their friends. He may not be mayor but he could still show people how things should be done.

A few days later, wanting to show Ada that he was as involved with the family as she and Nellie, he casually mentioned that he had the preparations for Kathleen's coming of age celebrations in hand. Instead of the look of pleasure which he had anticipated, he saw her look away and mutter something about talking to Nellie and Kathleen herself about it. As she retreated to the tiny scullery, she added something about London – her friends – not to go ahead with the invitations.

As there was no time for talking about private matters during shop hours, he waited until the evening and when the shop was closed he again brought up the subject. He could see in his mind's eye the party which he had planned, but he knew almost immediately that what the women had in mind was quite different.

'Sophisticated' was the word that kept coming up. 'Small,' they said, 'sophisticated,' they said and all those daft names that Kath's new friends had. Tommy had no idea of how to plan a party in London. But Kathleen knew exactly how it was done and it seemed a booking had already been made at Frascatis,

"Only provisional, Tom, only provisional," Nellie kept saying. But he knew differently. It was decided. He was to wear a dinner jacket and he was to behave. He was not to show Kathleen up in front of her friends. Ada was very firm on this point. Didn't he realise that some of Kathleen's friends were debs and one had a brother called Griffith Jones who was a matinee idol. He was somewhat relieved to hear it was the girl called Jonah; they called her that because her name was Miss Jones. Mr Griffith Jones was so popular that women sent him gifts. Jonah said that he had so many fur gloves sent to him by adoring women that he had some to give away and would Kathleen's young man like a pair? Everyone agreed that he was a very generous as well as good looking young man. Jonah said that he had been invited to go to Hollywood to become a movie star but he had declined. Even Tommy started to get interested in Kathleen's stories and he was secretly envious of all the stars she met when they came to be photographed at the Bond Street Studio.

One Thursday, after the shop had shut, Tommy decided to go secretly to London. He wanted to see where his daughter worked; he wanted to see why Ada always talked about London. He felt that he was somehow missing out and London was so near. So putting on his best suit, coat and hat and taking his silver-rimmed walking stick from the umbrella stand, he checked his moustache in the tiny mirror and walked to the station. It was nearing Christmas and he wanted to give Nellie something nice. He did give her a bad time, he had to admit it. Sometimes he couldn't believe how badly he spoke to her. He really wished she would stop him; yell back. Ada certainly would, at least he thought she would; he didn't know because he had never been so rude to Ada. He knew where he was going. Kathleen worked in Bond Street; that was where he would go. She was always talking about how wonderful the shops were in Bond Street. McIlroys and Butlers had nothing on the shops in Bond Street.

After he left the train at Paddington, and not wishing to get lost or to show his ignorance of the geography of the capital, Tommy entered one of the many taxis parked to the left of the platform and asked to be taken to Bond Street.

"Doing a bit of shopping guv'nor?" asked the cabbie. Tommy liked this reassurance that he was now perceived as a man of substance; a man who would naturally shop in one of the most prestigious streets in Europe. He wandered along the street, looking in admiration at not only the goods in the windows but also the appearance of the other shoppers. He began to see why young Kathleen liked to work there; he began to see why she had started to speak in the way that she did. Then he found it: Twenty, Bond Street. It was strange that they should live at Twenty-one, High Street, Maidenhead and Kath should work at Twenty, Bond Street.

He started to look into a shop nearby. It was full of glass; he recognised that it was the same sort of glass as the vase that Kath had bought her mother for her birthday – all swirly blues and violets. It was made to look as if there were irises growing up it. Nellie loved that vase. When Tommy looked closely at the tiny price tags, he could hardly believe his eyes; they made even Biggs look cheap. He turned to another man also studying the window and commented, "You wouldn't believe the prices, now would you?"

But his fellow window shopper merely lifted his shoulders and smiling answered with one word, "Lalique."

Tommy moved on still searching for a perfect gift. Now that he had seen where his daughter bought her presents for Nellie and realised the extent of her generosity, he felt he must find something that was just right.

He wandered into a large shop off Regent Street; he had gone in because it looked rather like a country house: timbered on the outside and with windows that were so beautifully dressed. Butlers had never managed to get their windows looking anything like this, even though Mrs Marks seemed to think that she was running a London store. No, this was real class; this was the real thing. He thought that he might get Kathleen to give him a few ideas about their own windows, though he had to admit that dressing a window with hams, bottles of cider and Camp coffee was not the same as dressing it with lengths of velvet, foreign carpets and magnificent umbrellas. That was it. There was his perfect gift. It was about a foot from his nose: a tall, elegant, quite magnificent lady's umbrella. It was not the sort of umbrella that a woman might take out on a showery day; not the sort of thing that someone might put into a shopping bag just in case.

This umbrella was something which a lady would take out in any weather. She could lean upon it, pose with it and flaunt it. It served the same purpose as a jewel. It told the world of wealth, status and the sort of functions that a lady might attend. He decided that this was the gift. It was perfect. He had seen old Queen Mary leaning on a similar one the last time that she had gone to Biggs. He would not even ask the price. He could just see Nellie in her Persian lamb coat and hat. He had always thought that something was missing and now he knew. It was an umbrella; this umbrella and he had found it. No matter what the cost, he would buy it.

He approached the counter and asked the sales lady if he might see the object of his interest. After it had been removed from the window, she laid it on the counter for his inspection and pointed out that the silk was an exclusive Liberty print and that the pommel of the handle was hall marked silver.

"No more than one would expect," murmured the lady, as if warning him that the price might be beyond his means. But Tommy had been looking in the windows. He was prepared and having been a horse trader at one time, he always carried a substantial 'reserve' in case an opportunity cropped up. Looking at the umbrella, he had the same feeling of wonder and awe that he always had when he came upon something special. The same feeling that had come over him when he first saw Nellie. He looked at the handle. It was circular and chased with a wonderful design and yet so smooth. A little small for his grasp but he knew it would fit Nellie's hand perfectly and the colours of the silk were subtle and the pattern echoed the design of the silver.

"I'll take it," he said quite simply and reached for his wallet.

"Would you like to know the price before you decide?" asked the assistant. It really was a very expensive item. But the customer simply repeated that he would have it and could it please be wrapped.

Having paid and picked up the gift by now superbly wrapped, Tommy remarked that he would look rather odd on his journey home carrying both a wrapped umbrella and his own silver banded walking stick. The lady then asked if he would like his purchase delivered and having heard that he lived in Maidenhead, she said that the store made frequent deliveries to the town and yes there would be no problem to deliver the article at all. Was it for Christmas or should it be delivered as soon as possible? Tommy was about to say just before Christmas but changed his mind and actually said,

"As soon as possible, and I should like to write a card."

He wrote quite simply, *'From your husband Tom.'* Then feeling quite elated, he made his way to Paddington and home. He caught a glimpse of Kathleen on the platform but she didn't see him. She was too busy chatting away to the young Bohemian.

The arrival of the gift was one of the high spots of Nellie's married life. It had not been bought as a bribe in the way that the ring had. It was for no special occasion and it was exactly what she would have chosen herself. It was simply quite wonderful and made her feel that no matter how often he shouted at her or tried to put her down in front of the customers and assistants, he did love her.

Strangely, the arrival of the umbrella brought out a jealous and previously unseen aspect of Ada's nature and she made Tom suffer for his generosity to his wife. The umbrella was to Ada like a red rag to a bull and Nellie was unable to enjoy the lovely gift as much as she might have. When it was delivered, she could hardly believe it. It was just so perfect and for some time afterwards she would give Tom little smiles across the shop when she thought of it.

Ada however, felt that she had been treated unfairly. She failed to realise that the gifts that Tom very, very occasionally bestowed on his wife were compensation for all the sorrow he had caused her. Ada also had a tendency to see everything that was Nellie's as her own and so for many years whenever a collection was being made of jumble or bric-a-brac, for the church or the guides, Ada would try to throw out the love gift that her sister cherished so much. Ada would bustle about muttering about lack of space, the flat being full of unused junk and then the umbrella would be found to be missing. For years Nellie managed to outwit her sister and retrieve the love token but eventually on one occasion, she was too late and the precious umbrella, one of the tenuous links between Tom and his wife, was gone. Ada maintained that it was broken, of no use and was prone to poke out people's eyes. But for once both Nellie and Tom were united in their thinking; Ada had known exactly what she was throwing out and to her sister and brother-in-law it was a great deal more than a wonderful umbrella.

Chapter 28

The Last Christmas

Christmas came first for the children. Some of the first children Tommy had taken gifts to were now grown up and with the factories opening in Slough many had got jobs and were starting to better themselves, moving away to rented accommodation. He could see so much of himself in so many of them; he hoped they would get on as he had. In the meantime, there were other children to help and he got on with raising the money and making the lists of boys and girls as he had for many years now. The vexed question of the gifts for men still came up from time to time but not from Nellie or Ada. So as the parcels were made up, there were still the groceries for the mothers, the toys for the youngsters and nothing for the men, just as in Miss Poupard's time.

In many ways the vast amount of money raised for that Christmas in 1937 was quite embarrassing. Even Tommy thought for a while that he should maybe weaken and put in a packet of cigars or razor blades for each of the men. But he had said he would not and now he could hardly go back on his word. He would look weak. He would look a patsy. So, he stood firm and as usual when he set off for the Barracks, no longer accompanied by Kath and Audrey, or Bunty as she was now known, he had nothing for the men.

His country ways, living close to nature and the animals may have given him a sixth sense for as he turned into the Barracks, a small shivery feeling went up his back. It was not the same this year. The children were not as excited and the women he had helped over the years looked embarrassed; they didn't smile in the same way. He could see the reason why. The entire male population of the area was there, lounging against the walls in the one bit of pale sunshine that had managed to find its way into the square. As he handed out the boxes, went through the now familiar chat of "What Father Christmas has for you," he felt an urgent need to get away. The male voices were at first a murmur but grew and he could make out,

"Nothing for us again then Tommy? I heard there was more money than ever from the raffle this year. Wonder where it all goes? No wonder old Tommy can keep buying houses. Where do you think the money comes from? Come the revolution, old Tommy and his likes will get their come-uppance."

There was laughter; unkind bitter laughter. He quickly unloaded the last of the boxes and climbing back onto the cart, he got the pony going and as he passed the jeering men he called out, "Well flick you then. This is the last year I do it. Do it yourselves you load of good-for-nothings."

And with that, not at all certain what reaction his retort would bring about, he touched the pony with the whip and shot out into Market Street at a dangerously high speed and completely failed to notice the vicar who was calling greetings to him from across the road.

When Tom told the family about his reception at the Barracks, much as they would have liked to have said, *"Well we told you so,"* none of them did. He was clearly upset and whatever criticisms may have been made of him, he certainly put a lot of effort and energy into this particular activity. Nellie said it would all blow over, but Ada secretly thought otherwise. She had thought for the last couple of years that it was time it all ended. Things were changing. People were not that desperately poor anymore and they neither wanted nor needed in most cases, charity from others. It was demeaning. She could see that. People wanted things by right; not handed out at the whim of people like Tommy. She had started to hear people say half-jokingly,

"Come the revolution…" Things were going to change in the coming years. They had to.

Chapter 29

The Anemone Elbow

Things had certainly changed for them. Ada could hardly remember her own twenty-first birthday. As she already had a baby by then, she probably spent it working but what a do Kathleen had been given. The older members of the family had been nervous at first of going into the London restaurant, but Kathleen had sailed in with her young man and soon everyone was laughing and at ease. Kathleen had looked wonderful in a chiffon dress printed with anemones, her mother's favourite flowers. It had been bought from the shop called Liberty's. Tom was never told what the frock had cost but it had certainly been a pretty penny. He didn't really mind. He wanted people to see that his daughter could go to the same shops as debs. He had worked to give all of them this sort of thing. The best; nothing but the best!

Money, he reflected, was the least important thing of all. Money was what you put in the night safe; it was the thing that made your fingers bleed if you didn't wear mitts and what wore out your trouser pockets. It was what you did with it: the houses you could acquire, the clothes you could buy for your women, the envy you could inspire in those who thought themselves better than yourself; that mattered.

There had nearly been a disaster the weekend before the party. Kath had gone over the handlebars of her bicycle and badly cut her elbow. She was dreadfully upset at the appearance of her arms and how the effect of the diaphanous gown would be ruined. But her young man had assured her that with or without scars, she would be the most beautiful woman there.

On the evening of the party, Maurice arrived with a box containing a corsage. This was usual for a grand or special event, but this was so thoughtful, so loving that it brought tears to the eyes of everyone present. Inside the box was a pad of anemones made by a skilled florist to tie with a violet satin ribbon around the elbow of a

153

lady; a lady with a badly cut elbow and a lady wearing a dress of chiffon flowers. Tommy could never have thought of something like that and he envied the young Bohemian as he glided around the room. This was what money could not buy. The young man might never make his fortune, but he was what Tommy would have liked to have been: talented and good looking; and a word he had overheard along the table, a romantic. That is what he would have liked to have been. But Tommy's parents had not eloped to France and his mother most definitely did not have the most beautiful voice in the county.

Watching his daughter dance, Tommy knew what it was he had been searching for: for glamour; for youth and for love. He had hardly come into contact with glamour; glimpsed it sometimes through the window of a carriage or seen it reclining in a punt on the Thames near Boulter's Lock. As for youth, he had had none. One moment he was in school and the next he was at work. Love, that too had eluded him, for neither of the middle-aged women sitting together across the table had ever really loved him. At least now he had touched these precious things. His children could dance and paint and play music. His daughter could drive a car and take photographs and his son could build wirelesses and mend motor cars. Without him, without his efforts, would they have managed all of this? Tears began to roll down the side of his face, partly in self-pity and partly for joy.

That was a wonderful year. Phil and Olive had their son and Kath and Maurice were engaged. The young people played tennis and went about in their little cars and on their motorbikes. The sun seemed to shine for months and months.

The Russian refugees had moved away – to Portugal someone said – and in their place came Jews from Germany. They told terrible tales of people disappearing; of strange camps that people dared hardly mention. Some people said that the Jews had always had something to moan about but others listened and said that Hitler needed to be stopped. A few of the older men said that sooner or later we would have to fight the Germans again.

On the home front, Mrs Simpson had pinched our King and the children sang,

'Sing, sing what shall we sing?
Mrs Simpson's pinched our king!'

154

The girls in the shop discussed at length how a middle-aged, plain and flat-chested American could steal the adorable Prince of Wales from under the noses of the bloom of the British debutantes. Older women spoke of dark arts which the American was said to have learned in Shanghai. Not one person was in any doubt that the Prince, the new King as he was now, had been led astray from his people. How could the son of Queen Mary and King George even think of it? A foreigner. A divorcee.

The world was going mad but strangely it was at this time that a certain calm came over the flat above the shop for they were all growing old and knew that nothing could now be changed. Even with the houses they had acquired, even with the money they had individually salted away, they had nowhere to go and none of them now wanted to.

Chapter 30

Patriarch

Both Tommy and Nellie thought there would be another war to go through. Another time of trial but neither ever doubted that England would prevail. Tommy said his prayer more fervently than ever and hoped that Phil and the young Bohemian would be spared. Had the old patriarch, for that is what he had become, known then what was to follow, he may well not have been as calm as he was as he approached the Christmas of 1938. Had he known that the family in a short while would be listening for news of the evacuation from Dunkirk, desperate that Phil might be picked up in one of the little ships, he would certainly have felt a sense of foreboding and dread.

The last Christmas before the lights went out over Europe and menace and horror were let loose among the vineyards of Italy and the villages of France, was a Christmas to savour and lay up in the moment. But as the last Christmas approached, he was glad that he had told the Barracks men that he would not be Father Christmas anymore. He was sure the time had come to stop the tradition anyway. He had kept his word to Miss Poupard for much longer than she could have anticipated and he was getting on. Someone else should do it; he would ask around.

The sound of crying reached them in the back room. It was Christmas morning but the bell was ringing and the doors and the windows were being knocked continually. Tommy attached his collar to the back of his shirt with a stud and went down the stairs into the shop. He had a sickening feeling that he knew who was at the door. And he was correct. All around the door were children; the children he should now be handing presents to. They smiled, thinking he had overslept and that he would soon be harnessing the pony and making his annual trip to see them with sacks of things to eat and play with in the cart. He tried to sound gruff and angry. He shouted that it was the fault of their ungrateful fathers but it just didn't come out like that. He looked at their faces. So few people had trusted him; but they had. He could only say, "I'm so sorry; I didn't know you wanted me to come." But those faces, used to poverty and hardship said it all. He had let them down; he had betrayed their trust and it was not their fault, it was his. His stupid temper had made him spoil the one really good thing he had done in his life. He was fifty-six and yet still the nasty little ferret popped out and made a fool of him; alienated friends and relatives. He missed the congratulations that he usually received after Christmas. He missed grubby little hands waving through the shop window and calling, "I know where Father Christmas lives." He could not look Mrs White in the face and the whole town seemed sadder somehow because of what he had failed to do.

An advertisement was placed in the Advertiser. It simply said that Father Christmas would be back next year and things would be better than ever. They never were. By next Christmas, Europe was at war.

On Black Friday Miss Jevons closed the studio in Bond Street where royalty, the stars and the socialites had gone to be photographed and where Kathleen had painstakingly extended the lashes of the likes of Evelyn Laye and removed moles and wrinkles from the photographs of worthy dowagers. The girls: Jonah, Dickie, Tony and Norah stood on the steps of St Pauls and vowed to meet there in ten years' time should they all survive.

Kathleen soon found work with her Maurice at High Duty Alloys on the Slough Trading Estate. They were part of the war effort: H.D.A. as they were known, making metals for aircraft. Later on, after they were married, they were sent to work at a shadow factory in Workington, Cumberland.

Both Kath and Maurice loved the Lake District and walking amongst the magnificent scenery but the Cumbrian natives were quite another matter. No-one was willing to take their ration books and Kath who was used to the best of food soon started to fade. Cumbrians could not bear the thought of Southerners taking any of their meagre rations and in time Kathleen was near to starvation – at one point pulling swedes from the fields and eating them raw. She had no wish to tell her mother or aunt just how dire the straits were. Luckily, she had dear Mrs Middleton as a char lady (as they were then called) who did her best to keep the delightful, if completely incompetent couple for whom she worked, alive.

One day, Kathleen was on the bus after work waiting for Maurice to join her. The two local girls behind her said one to another as Maurice approached, "You see that man there? They say he is quite mad and what is more they say his wife is as barmy as he is."

At about this time, Kath suspected that she may be expecting a baby. The lack of proper food was making her faint and ill and Ada and Nellie took the brave step of deciding to travel across wartime England to fetch Kathleen home. When they arrived, she fainted into her aunt's arms. The older women lost no time in returning with her to 21 High Street, Maidenhead where she was nursed and cossetted until her baby was born.

Soon after that, the theory of the girls on the bus was proved to have some truth as whilst supervising the night fire watch, Maurice decided to air the sleeping bags in front of an electric fire and set the whole factory alight. It was decided that Maurice was not perhaps cut out for a senior management position in wartime and he was directed to the recruitment office to join up.

Maurice was tall, blonde and blue-eyed. He spoke beautifully. The sergeant-in-charge decided on the strength of that, that Maurice was officer material. Shortly afterward he joined up in the R.A.F. and was sent to Cranwell where, to everyone's amazement, he became a pilot officer and flew Lancaster bombers. His timing was impeccable and by a sheer fluke he survived the war and went on to live until he was almost ninety-five.

Phil was less lucky. Although he too lived to a great age and died aged one hundred, he found himself at the start of the war in Dunkirk; that hell-hole from which an army was largely delivered by extraordinary bravery, courage, stoicism and good fortune.

The little boats of Maidenhead and their owners responded to the call for help to ferry the men from the beaches to the carrier ships moored off the coast of France. Although the Luftwaffe continually strafed them, the little boats went back and forth and an army was saved to fight on.

At home, in St Mary's, as in many towns across the country, the women prayed. Nellie, Ada and Kath prayed as they had never prayed before: for their sons, their lovers and the whole future of their country. They willed the Almighty to keep the waves down, to still the sea. As Nellie said with her deep Salvationist faith, "God did listen and young Phil and his mates got back." Phil said it was more to do with the fact that they were under the command of a regular sergeant and not some young university type. Whatever, back he came and everyone thanked God.

Everyone was concerned when Kathleen brought her baby back from the nursing home. How would Tom react to having a baby in the tiny flat? How would he cope with the crying; the nappies? After a few nights, Kathleen decided the baby must be left to cry; that was the modern method; no fussing or spoiling. Tom looked up several times pointedly in Kath's direction. After some time, he burst out, "If you don't pick up that poor flicking baby, then I will." And he did. It was the start of one of the closest relationships of his or the baby's life; his little Issy who grew up to follow him around to have *'A little bit of cheese Issy.'*

It was with Issy, Nellie, Ada and Kath that he watched the victory parade some two years later; when the war and all that it entailed had made old people of them.

"Look Issy, look! It's Monty!" he had shouted. But she had only seen Mr Bright, their window cleaner, marching along with the Home Guard.

Two years after that, Maurice had come home and little Issy with her white-blonde plaits and dark Badnell eyes had been taken from him.

Chapter 31

Leaving the Shop

Tommy frequently sang *'After the Ball was over'*, now it was *'After the war'*, the second war they had lived through. They all thanked the Good Lord that everyone in the family had come through alive. Phil came back from Burma half the weight he should have been and Kath had contracted a shadow on her lung as a result of living in Cumberland with little food. However, all in all they had survived and listening to many families, they knew just how fortunate they were.

'Good Old Winnie' whose photo graced the sideboard had led them through. But now, just as Ada had always thought, things were to change and new challenges faced Tommy and the family. For one thing, he was soon to retire and the flat where they had all lived for so long and from where they ran their various businesses, went with the job. Soon young Mr Abbott would be taking over and moving in above the shop with his wife and son.

Tommy and Nellie had always thought there would never be any difficulty in finding somewhere to live as they owned several houses. But all of these were occupied and new rental laws made putting out a long-standing tenant very difficult. They knew this because when Maurice had returned from the war and he and Kathleen and their two little girls had nowhere to go, they had to go to court to get out the tenants who lived in Beulah – Nellie's promised land that was to be her retirement home. Luckily, the tenants were unreliable payers and the house was dirty and anyway Maurice appeared in court in his RAF uniform and the magistrate declared that a war hero should be allowed a decent home; even more so as it was owned by the family.

But Mr Attlee was now in office and whilst his government did many excellent things, it made life hard for Tommy. He owned Canesaro but a family from the Channel Islands rented that and anyway their friend, Ada Leedell, rented two of the rooms. He was nearing his retirement and had nowhere to go. As he and Nellie went through the various houses they owned, there was not one that was suitable that they could move into.

One day, whilst visiting Kathleen in Fielding Road, Tommy took a walk and there, in the next road – Alwyn Road, the same road where Canesaro was situated– was a house with a 'FOR SALE' sign outside. He knew at once it was just what Nellie would love. It had leaded lights, an integral garage and a fish pond. When Nellie saw it, she knew it was the one; her heart was set on it. But the price – it was exorbitant. Tommy could not believe it. He had bought most of his property for hundreds not thousands. He would need to take out a mortgage, at his age. But it would be worthwhile. Nellie would have her large kitchen and leaded lights; he would have his shed and greenhouse and best of all, he would be a short walk from Issy, and better still the short walk passed a small off licence on the corner of Fielding and Alwyn Road.

How he had missed his little mate. Now he would see more of her; take her for walks, teach her about rabbits and birds and the trees and the weather. He would teach her the songs he knew and tell her to save her pennies and make herself safe. He didn't like the way his son-in-law and daughter treated her. They were harsh and aloof; more interested in their painting and violin playing than the poor kids and now Maurice had installed a great carpet loom in the kitchen! Thank goodness Ada was always round there: cooking, cleaning and ironing, as well as cuddling and looking after the poor little things. Funny how Kathleen was forever fainting and resting on washing days but always had strength to cycle to Cookham for her pottery and art lessons.

Tommy's retirement 'do' was not the affair it would have been before the war. Rationing had got worse but the Bell Hotel managed to put on a three course lunch with wine. Assistants past and present came including Norman Abbott, the new Manager. Head Office presented Tommy with a gold watch. Nellie and Ada were also given awards for their many years of service. Many people reflected on how much their unpaid work would actually have been worth, but these were the start of the socialist years. They had started when a woman was expected to help in her husband's work.

The move to Woodford Lodge was a great success. There was a front bedroom for Tom and Nellie and an attractive back bedroom

161

for Ada decorated with wallpaper of Chinese scenes and with a fireplace and an airing cupboard and a view of the garden. There was also a nursery which was soon occupied on a regular basis by Issy who joined in the games of whist they played with Ada Leedell a family friend who had become a permanent feature.

"We've seen the best of England," Tommy would intone, but the women knew those days had only been good for some. Ada Leedell had worked for a very rich man, someone called a stockbroker, who could afford more servants than were necessary. It was not the same for young women sent to houses where they were expected to do everything. Ada James, or Nanny as she was now known to avoid confusion with Ada Leedell, knew that.

The great joy for Tommy was walking the dog with his little mate. Behind the house, before Courthouse School was built, the fields were full of flowers: poppies, cornflowers and scabious and tobacco plants. Tommy pointed them all out to his granddaughter and pointed to the skylarks high in the clouds. They would leave Woodford Lodge, taking Spot the dog on his lead, and turn right at Old Mrs Baldwin's house where they reached the alleyway that led past the prefabs, with their fitted kitchens and bathrooms and that were quite the envy of many housewives. They passed the caravan park in the corner and the site where the new school was to be built and onto the fields where Spot was let off the lead and would rush about ecstatically.

"Look, he's our little whippet" Tommy would say, remembering his own whippets of long ago.

They played games to see if there were pictures in the clouds and as she got older they went further – onto the Thicket where at one time there had been footpads who robbed travellers using the Old Bath Road. Once they had strayed near to Pinkney's Green and a very charming man left his garden to speak to them. He was intrigued by the old man and the little girl. Tommy didn't know who he was but Issy did. When they moved on she said,

"Grandad, don't you know who that is? It's Richard Todd, he is really, really famous. He's just made a film called *'The Dam Busters'.*" She knew this because the famous film star had very kindly come and presented prizes at the brownies' end of year party.

Poor little Issy went cross-eyed. Kathleen said it was because she had been knocked over by a bicycle but Tommy knew differently. The child was unhappy. Like him, she would have liked to be back at home at the shop. He never saw Maurice pick her up or ruffle her hair. He never heard Kathleen speak to Issy as Nellie did. His other granddaughter, Janet (Phil's daughter) reported that Auntie Kath slapped poor Isobel around the face for saying that she didn't like the dinner. Phil's wife Olive was a strict mother but a very loving one and she would never have done such a thing. No wonder Issy went boss-eyed.

"I'm going to leave Kath's share to Issy," said Tom.

"You do that and they will make the child's life hell," replied Ada.

"They do anyway," he muttered.

The poor child had chilblains and everyone said how cold the house was. Tom told the coal man to drop off a few hundredweight of coal and put it on his bill. He was also concerned about Issy's baby sister Carrie, the litte'un or Nipper. She, it seemed, had a 'mysterious illness'. It wasn't a mystery to Tom. He felt very defensive of the poor little flickers. Ada explained that Kathleen was preparing her girls for when the Russians came. She was endlessly going on about the Russians, mixing with all those Bolshie arty types at Cookham; all barmy.

In time, Nellie gave Beulah to Kath and Maurice so that they could build their dream house, Willow Tarn, at Hawthorn Hill. It took the girls away from their friends and family as the only connection was the Bray bus. Kathleen was in seventh heaven but Kathleen throughout her long life invariably had what she wanted. The fact that it was just as cold as Beulah did not affect her and that the girls had no friends did not occur to her. She had her house on the hill and a studio. What more could anyone want?

But Tommy had taught Issy a lot. Not only about the Berkshire countryside he loved so much but to 'put a little away for a rainy day' and that, 'if you look after the pennies the pounds will take care of themselves'. He also advised Issy to become a teacher. He thought of the war widows he knew from both wars.

"You be a teacher Issy," he said, "If you are ever left, you'll be alright. You'll have a pension."

There were other things he taught her like telling the time from the sun and the way to find your way home is to close your eyes and think of it and then follow the way your instinct tells you. Most importantly he told her often and with great meaning how much he loved her and would always be there for her.

Epilogue

Inevitably the link between Tommy and Issy loosened but it was there for all time. There was so much to keep the bond strong. Each day Tommy's shoe horn eased on her shoes and beside her bed she kept a snuff box that reminded her that although her Grandfather may well have become a disgusting old man in later life, he had carried her home from the Old Time Dance singing *"You should see me dance the Lancers, it's the prettiest dance I know."*

Issy was given the two oval pictures that Old Walter had bought by her mother Kath. She frequently studied them when they hung on her bedroom wall. She often pondered if they had reached the place where things were as they should be and if at last they were young and carefree; gazing from open windows to greet their great loves. She did hope so.

When she was about eighteen, Issy was watching Helen, as Nellie came to be known by her correct name after her retirement, sitting at her dressing table. Helen was always most particular about her skin care and told her granddaughter to use Pond's cold cream followed by Pond's vanishing cream to take away the shine. Everyone agreed Helen always had beautiful skin, when her eczema was not playing up. The older woman felt at the back of drawer and suddenly said "You had better have this, I will never wear it." And she told her granddaughter the story of the old Russian lady with whom she had played cards all those years ago. The cross looked old and rather brassy but Issy wore it on religious occasions and after the baptism of her son Alex she noticed the settings of the brooch were loose and sent it to Hatton Garden from where it emerged as the sparkling jewel the old Russian lady would have recognised. On her seventieth birthday Carrie was given the beautiful jewel by her sister in recognition of the love, and loss she felt for her. She sometimes envied Ada and Helen, they had always had each other and the love of two sisters can be very strong.

After her death Kath's two daughters, Issy and Carrie inherited boxes of beads and trivia, piles of instructions and books marked

READ THIS!!! It was from one of the packets of papers that the name Miss Poupard emerged and the fact that she ran a very high-class dress shop, Issy hoped she was more accurate in these facts than she had been in many.

Among the beads Issy found a twisted piece of metal that a Billericay Jeweller declared to be twenty-two carat gold, hallmarked in nineteen twenty-seven. He remade it and Issy is constantly reminded as she twists it on her finger that sometimes even now if women want the best they have to get it for themselves, another lesson to pass on.

From time to time Issy wonders if she will ever get her ancestors out of her head. Each time she visits her son, there in a sparkling modern kitchen sits a bent cane chair that came from the shop. It is now a vivid yellow and belongs more in a Van Gogh painting than a grocer's shop, but memories, they are all around. She has only to glimpse the chair and she can see the rest of the scene the chair belongs to: the shelf above where the Camp coffee bottles were stacked, with the man wearing a kilt; the long wooden counter with pretty Doreen and her Grandma standing behind it. Maybe she should round up all the memories and shut them up in a book, only to be allowed out when people wished to meet them. But was that what she really wanted? They had kept her company for so long and often seen her through her darkest hours.

Issy did become a teacher and did save her pennies. She moved to Billericay in Essex, a town much like Maidenhead with its bustling High Street, its jewellers and sense of comfortable prosperity. She now shares her old age with a retired London Black taxi driver who has many similarities to Tom, so she remembers to cuddle him and tell him how wonderful he is. Together, they walk with their grandchildren and point out the trees, the flowers, the birds and the insects. At Southwold, Issy declared as they walked on the beach,

"I must go down to sea again, to the lonely sea and the sky," a poem she had learnt at school and always loved.

Walking through the Chestnut trees in Norsey Wood (a fitting entry to the hereafter she always thought) with the shafts of almost theatrical sunlight streaming through the broad-leafed canopy above, she could not help but shout out her favourite of all time poem,

"Praise be to God for dappled things, for skies of couple-colour as a brinded cow."

It was different from old Tommy singing *Two little girls in blue lad, two little girls in blue.*

Most important of all, Issy often tells her granddaughter how much she loves her and that she will always be there for her.

"What would you do if I got lost?" asked the child.

"I would find you," Issy replied.

"What if I was a long, long way away?"

"Then I would send someone to find you, I would always find you, I love you so much."

Issy had the feeling that once, somewhere, maybe on Maidenhead Thicket she had had a similar conversation. Only this time, she was not the child, she was the grandparent.

The child smiled up at her laughing, and Issy had the warm feeling that somewhere, maybe some way off, Tommy, Nellie and Ada were watching... and they were smiling too.

About the Author

Isobel Greenshields hails from Berkshire and spent the first four years of her life with her grandparents at 21 High Street, Maidenhead. Later she attended Windsor Grammar School and Ranelagh School in Bracknell. She first lived in Essex during her teaching training. She taught for thirty years and was once described as *'a born story-teller'*. In 2010 she won first prize in an Age Concern story writing competition and was co-ordinator for her local U3A's Poetry and Creative Writing Group. Isobel intends to publish more family stories and write her own eventful life story.

25535218R00101

Printed in Poland
by Amazon Fulfillment
Poland Sp. z o.o., Wrocław